If You Fall

Karen Darke

Winchester, UK
Washington, USA)

First published by O Books, 2006
O Books is an imprint of John Hunt Publishing Ltd.,
The Bothy, Deershot Lodge, Park Lane, Ropley, Hants, SO24 0BE, UK
office1@o-books.net
www.o-books.net

Distribution in:
UK and Europe
Orca Book Services
orders@orcabookservices.co.uk
Tel: 01202 665432 Fax: 01202 666219 Int. code (44)

USA and Canada
NBN
custserv@nbnbooks.com
Tel: 1 800 462 6420 Fax: 1 800 338 4550

Australia
Brumby Books
sales@brumbybooks.com
Tel: 61 3 9761 5535 Fax: 61 3 9761 7095

Singapore
STP
davidbuckland@tlp.com.sg
Tel: 65 6276 Fax: 65 6276 7119

South Africa
Alternative Books
altbook@peterhyde.co.za
Tel: 27 011 792 7730 Fax: 27 011 792 7787

Text copyright Karen Darke 2006

Design: Stuart Davies

Front cover picture of the author on the Zinal Rothorn, Swizterland 1992,
copyright Alun Powell.

ISBN-13: 978 1 905047 88 8
ISBN-10: 1 905047 88 6

The rights of Karen Darke as author have been asserted in accordance with the Copyright,
Designs and Patents Act 1988.

A CIP catalogue record for this book is available from the British Library.

Printed in the US by Maple Vail

If You
Fall

Karen Darke

BOOKS

Winchester, UK
Washington, USA

ACKNOWLEDGEMENTS

This is with thanks to my parents, Mike & Chris Darke.
And for Will Ramsbotham, good friend and climbing partner.
I offer my heartfelt thanks to all the friends, acquaintances and
strangers who have shown me so much kindness and enabled me
to live and experience this journey.
Particular thanks to Robin Shohet and Matthew Ferguson who
have coached and supported me with such insight and patience in
writing this book.
Thank you also to Suresh for his love and support.

CONTENTS

FOREWORD

When individuals take great risks and attempt great endeavours, they will need to test themselves and draw on their inner reserves of strength. Often, back at home, such people can act the more effectively in every day life as a result of their experiences "on the edge".

Karen knows this better than anyone. She fell, heart breakingly so. But out of this she has found a strength and resilience that she probably didn't realize she had before, and which most of us don't get anywhere near. And her story is not just one of the triumph of the human spirit, but of the 'spiritual'. It's 'spirit' that makes us what we are, 'spirit' that calls out to us in the wilderness places.

This isn't just a book about physical survival, about coming to terms with a broken body, but of finding the 'spirit' within all of us, whether we're out on the mountains or at home in the living room. It's about crossing that fine borderline between what seems real and what seems impossible. Read this to understand what drives people like Karen, but more importantly to make the connections yourself between where you are now and where you could be.

RANULPH FIENNES

PROLOGUE

FALLING

"Life can only be understood backwards; it has to be lived forwards."

SØREN KIERKEGAARD

At some point in life, we are likely to fall. By 'fall' I mean that something happens to us that we find challenging to deal with. It might be a sudden, unexpected event that catapults us into the chaos of personal crisis. Or perhaps we are drifting along on the currents of life, feeling like something needs to change but not quite knowing how or what to do about it.

My 'big' fall happened when I was twenty-one. I was paralysed in a rock-climbing accident. That's nothing unique – this kind of crisis happens to lots of people in all kinds of ways. This was the event that stopped my life as I'd known it, and set me on an extraordinary journey from the brink of death to hand-cycling in the Himalaya and to the rusty knife of a Brazilian spirit surgeon. These adventures have catalysed an inner journey that make me question what is real, to wonder about the patterns of beliefs that surround us, and to get to know myself in relation to the world in a way that I would never have thought possible.

I have been fortunate to travel, to be able to explore within whilst exploring outwith, but I don't believe we necessarily need to go 'out there' to do this. The biggest explorations of ourselves often happen on our own doorsteps. One of my biggest explorations occurred whilst lying in a bed staring at a ceiling for two months. But I am a person who is stimulated by the world around me, rather than from within. I get my ideas, my motivation and my inspiration from 'out there', and that is why I have been compelled to journey and travel in order to discover. You may wonder as you read, "How on earth did she manage to go to all these places?" It may all sound rather exotic and 'surreal', and often it felt that way to me too. I'm not rich, but I am resourceful. I'm lucky enough not to be scared of roughing it and I've also met with incredible kindness. It is thanks to all of this that so many of my adventures have been possible.

When I was thrown from my rather comfortable place in life, I found it cathartic to write and to express the spaghetti of feelings tangled within me about being paralysed. The anonymity of a piece of paper allowed me to express what it was like not being able to walk, climb mountains, run, dance, play – or at least not in the way I'd been used to. However, writing this book is the scariest thing I have ever done – more so than any physical adventure I could ever dream up. It has asked me to share a part of me that normally stays hidden.

Good memories are wonderful things to have, but they can hold us back too. For years I wrangled with my own waves and whirlpools of emotions, haunted by memories of the past and what I used to be able to do. But as my internal storm slowly subsided, I became happy and more engaged with the world around me again. I began to realize that when I met new people, something about my very visible disability, the fact that I was young and active, and had been shunted into something that people found hard to comprehend, seemed to catalyse a torrent of thoughts and emotions for them. I was regularly bombarded with questions, or confronted with inquisitive faces, asking, "What happened to you? How do you 'cope'? How would I cope if it happened to me? Why aren't I doing more with my life whilst I still can?" Sometimes these are asked directly but often people are too embarrassed and I read the questions on their faces.

"Why do I seem to cause this response?" I wondered. It seems that my situation, and something about having a disability but remaining active, ignites in people memories of their own near-misses, sparks of regret for the things they should do before they might not be able, reflection on their life and its missed opportunities and questioning of their own resilience. Why does it so often take a fall, our own or another's, in whatever shape or form, to cause us as humans to 'wake up' to who we are and how we are living?

For most, personal 'disaster' creeps up on us, and at some point we wonder what it is all about. It might be a mid-life crisis; a career upset; a dysfunctional family or relationship, or like me, becoming paralysed. Often we don't reflect on our lives, we are barely conscious, until something causes us to fall down. Then we are swept out to a stormy sea on a rip tide, forced to come to terms with what's happened, as if a giant salty wave has unexpectedly crashed over our head. We are forced to consciously consider ourselves and our lives.

Here I share my story, of being active, or hyperactive, with a disability, and maybe it will just be a story for you, or maybe it will ignite latent sparks and cause you to live your life listening to the quiet voices inside you, rather than waiting for an unexpected explosion to catalyse change.

CHAPTER 1

FREE FALL FROM LIFE

"When the morning's freshness has been replaced by the weariness of mid-day, when the leg muscles quiver under the strain, the climb seems endless, and, suddenly, nothing will go quite as you wish...."
'The Climb Seems Endless', MARKINGS

"I'd rather be dead than paralysed", I said, not really believing that either were ever likely to happen to me.

I was recounting the story of a family friend as our small group cycled back from an evening out. He had been thrown over the handlebars of his bike when a loose mudguard got tangled with his wheel. He was paralysed from the neck down. "I can't imagine anything worse" I said. "Just think of not being able to move anything." We pulled grimacing faces and shook our heads at the prospect. One friend promised to tighten the loose mudguard I'd noticed on his bike. We said goodnight, parted and cycled off in our separate directions, in search of our beds and some warmth from the bone-biting damp of a fading Scottish winter. "I'd rather be dead than paralysed," I thought again briefly as my bike wheel rattled over the cobbles towards home.

Eight hours later, breakfast was interrupted by the peep of a car horn. Cramming down my remaining banana, I grabbed my rucksack stuffed full of climbing gear and ran outside. It was a bright March morning, the sun insisting that it still existed after a winter in hibernation. It was deceivingly cold, and Pete, Isla, Mark and Scott waited in a cozily full car. I squeezed into the back seat, and we set off, randomly turning at junctions with typical indecision about where to go climbing for the day.

"North or south?" Mark asked. After a few laps of Aberdeen's Beach Boulevard, we reckoned that the sky to the south looked more reliable than the ominous grey already building to the north. With a decisive U-turn, we aimed for the cliff-clinging commuter village of Cove. I'd never climbed there before, but gathered after a few months in Aberdeen that it was a reputed spot.

We parked along a dirt track, grass grown high along the centre. The car boot was a nest of brightly coloured sacks, clothes, ropes and gear. Taking turns to grab our things, we set off along the path towards the cliffs and after a short walk, scrambled our way carefully downward, picking a safe route to the rocky platform below. There was a shelf of rock at the bottom of the cliffs, perfect as a base for the day. The sea was calm and the brightness blinding. I turned to the rock and inspected the routes above.

We took a while to match the description of the climbs in the guidebook to what we could actually see at the rock-face. We flicked through the pages, reading about the routes and their grades. I'd heard that some of the routes on these cliffs were very worn, the once grippy rock and sharp pits and corners having become rounded and polished from wear by a constant stream of climbers. We split into two groups and began – Pete, Scott and Isla starting a route just to the right of Mark and me.

"Shall I lead?" Mark asked. "I'd like to give it a try" I replied with an expression that added "If that's okay with you". It was only graded a 'HVS' (Hard Very Severe), which is, though the words might be deceiving, not that difficult in climbing terms.

I made hard work of the first section of the climb, clutching and grabbing at the polished overhanging rock, my arms throbbing as their muscles burned with lactic

Climbing Pierre & Rabboutez, Aiguille du Midi, Chamonix, August 1991

acid. My chest pounded and fear ran through my veins as I grabbed feverishly at the smooth rock above a bulge that pushed into my stomach. I found a grip with my hand and a tiny lip with my foot, enough to pull myself through to the easier-angled rock above. I panted with relief, jammed a piece of climbing gear into the rock and clipped the rope in. Safe!

I relaxed for a minute and let the life seep back into my arms, shaking them gently at my side, one at a time. I noticed the waves breaking against the rocks below me and the sounds of the gulls squawking overhead, the rock dribbled in their crusty white debris. I could see the others, bright shapes on the cliffs a few hundred metres away, their shouts to each other reduced to muffles on the breeze. I wondered whether to back-off and let Mark's enormous biceps make light-work for us, but I hated to give up.

Some strength oozed back into my arms again and I began to pick my way up the gentle incline. I could see that the route traversed right towards a bulging nose of rock, before continuing upwards to the top. The rock quickly steepened and its dull grey-green glassy texture added to my trepidation. I focused on moving sideways, and very carefully, one small move at a time, I edged slowly to my right.

My hands felt greasy against the cold rock, the angle becoming steeper with every step sideways. Beads of sweat showed my fear and my muscles shook with fatigue – climbers call it 'disco leg' - but I had disco arms too. My grip weakened and I felt the energy flow from my arms and fingers, faster and faster, like water accelerating down a drain.

I called to Mark, warning him to take in the slack rope. I had taken a lead fall only once before, at a quarry close to my Yorkshire home. On that occasion, my legs and arms had turned to jelly. I'd dripped more than just beads of fear-induced sweat, and when my fingers had finally lost all functionality, I'd let out a pathetic yelp in expectation of a long fall. My arms had flown backwards into nothingness, and I had become airborne, a mixture of fear and adrenaline surging inside. Incredibly, before my mind had a chance to register the situation, my feet had collided with the rock face and I'd stopped abruptly. The gear had held tight and my dramatic swing down had left me in a peaceful pendulum.

I could hear the panic in my own voice as I called to Mark.

"Here I am again," I thought. "Shit."

My mind was rigid with fear. "Hold on," I told myself. I felt terror flood through me as I realized that I didn't have a scrap of strength left. I watched my fingers, as if in slow motion, slide from the rock.

An instant later I plummeted from the cliff, and into a void.

I don't remember anything.

No pain.

Nothing. Just darkness.

According to Mark, seeing me fall had a dreamlike quality. He watched me falling for an infinite few seconds to the rocky platform below. The implications of such a trivial slip were so huge, that he felt it couldn't be happening.

When I hit the ground he assumed I was dead. I was lying in a horribly twisted, crumpled way, as if I'd been hit by a fast lorry. My wrists were pushed back and skewed, the bone showing white through the skin. It looked like a big flap of my skull had just been removed. There was a lot of blood, and on coming close Mark realized I wasn't breathing. He opened my mouth and moved my tongue. I took a big, gurgling slow breath, and then time seemed to speed up.

Everyone rushed around. Pete ran to a house on the edge of the village to call for help. As life ebbed from me, it seemed to him that he could never reach the houses quick enough. It felt like an eternity but was actually only minutes before he was explaining the incident and location to the emergency services. The others were cutting ropes, trying to support my head and body, doing all these efficient things on autopilot.

The panic of the situation became engulfed by an eerie calmness as they sat, helpless, fearing that any attempt to move my damaged body might cause further injury. There was nothing else to do except cover me for warmth. They waited for help to arrive,

Cosmiques Arete, Aiguille du Midi, Chamonix, August 1991

mulling the practicalities of a rescue from the awkward, cliff- and sea-caged location.

Relief brimmed when the paramedics arrived. It wasn't easy to decide on the best method of moving my limp body from its unhelpful location. It would be difficult to carry me up the steep cliff scramble, but tricky also for the coastguard boat that bobbed offshore to safely approach the rocky coast. A helicopter arrived shortly afterwards and an air rescue was chosen as the safest route.

The yellow wasp buzzed overhead with a paraphernalia of ropes dangling below. Paramedics strapped me to a stretcher and tied it to the ropes. The chaos on the ledge was a stark contrast to the school of dolphins gliding through the calm ripples in the bay, sunlight reflecting from their fins. I vaguely remember the whirring helicopter blades, and my stomach turning as I was swung upwards. My only other recollection of the trauma was shouting my parents' postcode, over and over.

HX7 2PY!!! HX7 2PY!!! Then nothing.

Mark, Pete, Isla and Scott walked back to the car, very slowly and in silence.

I plunged into two days of unconscious ignorance, a distressing interim for my family and friends, as I teetered on the tightrope of life. My blood oxygen levels recorded the battle, once plummeting so low that I was almost gone. Mark, Pete, Isla and Scott waited uncomfortable hours in Accident and Emergency, anxious to hear the outcome of my battle. An informative policeman, closely followed by a discretion-less reporter, arrived on Mum and Dad's Yorkshire doorstep, initiating their long drive north. My brother Simon abandoned his studies and caught the train to Scotland.

When I eventually opened my bloodshot eyes, Mum and Dad's faces were there, relieved eyes looking down at me, my foggy mind just active enough to register their presence.

Mark, Pete, Isla and Scott found out I was conscious and talking and they felt a huge weight of fear lift from them. They thought "She's going to be okay. Another climbing story, another close scrape for embellishment down the pub." The next day they arrived in intensive care wearing ridiculous white plastic aprons. It seemed a great, flashing, shining, alien room. They'd thought of things to say. Some jokes. Some stories about the helicopter. They weren't prepared to see me looking like an animal in an experiment, my personality caged and hidden behind injuries and technology, my mouth stuffed with a hideous tube for oxygen. Words were lost.

In the seracs, Feegletscher glacier, Alphubel, Switzerland, July 1991

Mark told me that after that day, his whole perspective on life changed. Everything he did seemed pathetically trivial and self-indulgent. He had a terrible feeling of powerlessness, that this stupid, unimportant, infinitesimal moment on a rock face could have done this, and that there was nothing anyone could do to change it. We all wished we'd driven north instead of south that day. Mark wished that he had led the climb. I wished I hadn't been so stubborn and that I had let him.

My life changed so dramatically in a few seconds that day, 14 March 1993. I wonder how many of us carry significant dates hidden within us, a symbol of when life changed?

CHAPTER 2

A NEW REALITY

"What doesn't kill me, makes me stronger."
ALBERT CAMUS

I was faced with a new reality. My view of the world was distorted, lying flat on my back. A metal halo was drilled into my skull. From it hung kilogram weights to keep my spine in alignment. I stared at the ceiling. My body felt numb and tingly as if I'd just lain on my arm too long while asleep, sending it dead and robbed of sensation. Normally the tingles get more and the numbness less as the blood and the life slowly seep back into your arm. But after a few minutes of consciousness, my numbness was persisting. A white coat appeared at my bedside and straining my eyes sideways I met the eyes of a doctor. I beat him to speech.

"So what's the story?" I invited frankness.

"You are paralysed. The extent of the damage to your spinal cord isn't certain, so it's possible that you may recover some movement, but unlikely that you will be able to walk. Your injuries are extensive – in addition to a chest-level break in your spine, you have an unstable break in your neck. It is critical that we immobilize your neck to prevent damage to the spinal cord there, which would lead to loss of arm movement. You also have multiple fractures of the wrist, elbow, ribs and skull..." He continued, but I was no longer listening. The consultant was frank with everyone, almost ruthless, describing my injuries and prospects for recovery as if he was reading from a medical textbook. I suppose he knew there were no words that would make it sound better and I appreciated his straightforward approach.

In an instant, my life had changed. I was paralysed. The world around me was no different, yet to me nothing was the same. I showed no tears or visible distress. My senses were numbed by whatever medication I had been dosed with. The insular world of intensive care was a drugged blur. White coats came and went. Kind voices spoke and disappeared. The ceiling stayed, staring blankly down at me. White plastic tiles with a pitted effect, some with stains and marks. "How do ceiling tiles get stained and damaged?" I wondered.

My eyes roamed sideways and I could just see the wall where it met the ceiling. It was pale green. The more I analyzed it, for variety from the white tiles, the more sickly its shade appeared. Who decides to paint hospitals these dismal colours? Cold colours like pale green and blue. I tried to think of a better colour; I couldn't. Red or orange were less non-descript, but then you'd go mad staring at their brightness all day. Lemon or pink would be even worse. Sunshine yellow perhaps. That would be cheery. Or perhaps the white tiles, with their pits for interest, weren't so bad after all.

Lower down the green wall, too far in my peripheral vision to actually focus on it, was the corner of a window. When I detected the rich blue of the sky, I thought of the world outside. I thought of all the people that I knew, acting out their daily routines. I could hear traffic. I thought of the sea that I was sure I would see if I could stand at the window. I contrasted all the activity out there with my few cubic metres of space; my life centrifuged by that short but devastating fall, into a cocooned existence.

I thought of all that I had left behind, outside those four walls, and wondered if and when I would return to that life. My desk and its piles of books and papers at the University, where I was studying for a geology PhD; my student flat and tiny room, so small that I had to store my mountain bike under the bed; my friends at the Triathlon club and our regular runs and jaunts to the pub; weekends piling into a minibus with student friends and zipping off to the mountains. I thought of all the things I missed. My life suddenly seemed such a happy, active, normal life in comparison to the one I was being confronted with. I craved for it back again. I wanted normality.

Before my mind could wander any deeper into my lurking despair, I dragged my thoughts back to my surroundings and tried to focus again on the monotonous view above, and was thankful when the next visitor arrived to distract me.

As my senses started to sharpen and life around me gained some clarity, I felt a wave rising through my body. It was a sign that a doctor or nurse had visited the base of my bed, just out of my range of sight, and injected more diamorphine into my feet. It was hard to imagine that someone could stick a big needle into my body and that I couldn't feel it.

The brief episodes of near-alertness between drugged hazes became appealing. It was frustrating not to be able to hold a sensible conversation with anyone that came to visit, and the last thing I wanted was a morphine addiction. I started to object to the doses of mind-fuzzing drugs, desperate to speak to people, to start to make sense of what had happened.

Slowly, periods of lucidity increased, and the white coats gained faces and personalities. Some of the nurses and doctors were fantastic to me. The hospital food was so unappealing and my weight so quickly diminishing, that one nurse even bought me Marks & Spencer's meals and prepared them for me specially. I looked forward to her shifts! Another spent hours telephoning Aberdeen hairdressers, in search of some kind of super-conditioner that would help them detangle my matted mess of hair rather than having to shave it off. They somehow understood the importance of these small things in helping me stay mentally together. Shaving my hair off would have felt like a final loss of the life I remembered, like Samson losing his mane.

A human grapevine had been buzzing with news, so the harsh reality of my circumstances was softened by distraction from a constant stream of friends. I valued the hours they spent with me, and the appearance of old friends I hadn't seen for a long time. Friends and family were my lifeline. I couldn't have weathered the force of the explosion without them.

My appetite was poor, but Mark, Pete, Isla and Scott visited daily with treats of fruit and yogurt. They dropped missiles of grape and yogurt dollops from above, which I tried to catch in a gaping mouth. With no neck or head movement possible, the yogurt splattered on the sheets and I had to retrieve grapes from folds in the bedclothes. In my new restricted world, small entertainments were welcome.

It felt to them grotesquely unfair, almost obscene, that they were just carrying on with their lives, whilst mine had changed so much. When they visited, they felt a great pressure to be happy and positive. I didn't want misery, so they were all up beat, although often I think everyone just felt like screaming "This is a fucking nightmare!"

I was still living in my dreams, reality just a movie reel I occasionally awoke to, my bed and the surrounding few metres the only set I ever saw. I spoke little with anyone about what had happened. I am sure my friends and family spoke amongst themselves. Everyone was finding their own way of adjusting. Mum and Dad were occupying their hours with trips to the coffee shop and visitor entertainment. I didn't discuss paralysis with anyone. There were too many other more immediate issues to reconcile, like my dangerously low blood oxygen levels, the lung drain tapping into my chest, and the two plastered arms that left me limbless. My conversations were mostly general chitchat about what was happening outside those four walls. A drugged haze and denial kept me sane.

My view of the ceiling improved with some colourful posters strategically stuck in my line of sight. There was one of some Himalayan mountains in Pakistan and another of a polar scene with icebergs floating in a bay. The printed colours were too filtered and false to conjure realistic images in my mind, and I was too drugged to feel upset about never visiting mountains and wild places again. Bizarrely, it was almost fun lying there, regally crowned in the ugly black halo, whilst friends I hadn't seen for months, even years, appeared at the bedside. When daylight faded, so did the visitors. I was left alone with a cocktail of drugged thoughts, and my dreams.

I lie alone, on top of a rocky tor, staring up at the sky, mesmerized by the fast moving cotton wool clouds. The cold hardness of the rock is soothing. I visit Bennachie often, to admire the view of the distant mountains, to wander through the heather, and to think. It is a blustery March day and the wind is chilling on the skin but I barely notice.

Stirring out of a thoughtful trance, I slowly clamber to my feet. I bend down to tighten the laces of my shoes, stretching my calf muscles simultaneously, then rise and contemplate the route down. Over to the left are three more tors, surrounded by blossoming heather, with well-trodden, narrow paths winding along the ridge between them. Below them, the forest creeps up from the valley, and I can just glimpse the River Don, twisting through the trees and glimmering in the sunlight. The beauty of Scotland fills my lungs, and a slow run jolts my muscles into action; I begin the route along the ridge.

Quickening pace, my blood pumps faster and my head pounds. Breathing deeply, I concentrate to keep up with myself. My thoughts start to dissolve, until my mind becomes blank and relaxed. The only sounds are of the wind, of my feet impacting on the dry peaty earth, and the whistle of breath.

Ten minutes later I enter the forest. At the edge of the trees, gorse and daisies colour the ground. The path, carpeted in pine needles, bends ahead towards a dark wooded heart. The trees play with the sunlight, soft golden shadows flicker onto the damp ground. Breathing the forest air, the aroma of pine invigorates and refreshes my tired mind. Briefly I leave the path, urgently running through dense trees, branches whipping my face and my feet occasionally sliding on musty roots. I emerge from the trees into the gravel of the car park, collapse against a bench and close my eyes, breathing deeply to recover. Wind through the trees tricks light across my eyelids.

I opened my heavy eyes, and in place of the trees, daylight filtered around the blind, the hospital window a dark silhouette. Reality encroached; a shocking nightmare. My world of dreams was far more appealing.

My head itched. My left elbow and right wrist set in plaster and a numb useless right hand drove me crazy. Even if I could scratch, I dared not for fear of what my fingertips might find – the expressions on my visitors' faces disturbed me. My suspicions were confirmed when one friend fainted upon seeing me, keeling over at the bedside into the bleeping boxes to which I was connected. After a while, I decided I should confront myself and asked for a nurse to hold a mirror above me.

A stranger stared back. A bolt protruded from either side of my skull, supporting a half-inch metal crown from which weights hung somewhere out of sight. My hair, I remembered as being long and blonde, was dark, matted with old blood, shaven around the bolts, while a deep stitched scar dissected my forehead from my crown. My skin looked pallid and drawn and unfamiliar eyes had replaced the normal blue-grey. They were bloodstained, like a bullet-shot on glass, with rainbows of bloody black-blue-purple exploding from the sockets to my temples.

Quietly, I asked the nurse to remove the mirror. Quickly!

For the first time, a lonely tear spilled from the corner of one eye.

After a month in intensive care, I was informed that I would be transferred to a specialized spinal injuries unit at Pinderfields Hospital in Yorkshire. The journey would not be safe, I was told, with my neck in its unstable state. The neural surgeon would drill more holes into my skull to fix the latest fashion in headgear. It would apparently ensure that any jarring movements in transport would not damage my neck. More giant needles – a cocktail of local anaesthetic into my forehead, and the ultimate morphine fix into my feet. A giant tidal wave washed upwards, engulfing my mind and sending me into a land of gibberish. I remember my forehead being doused in bright yellow iodine, and then a drill. My brother, Simon, was at my side, his sweaty hand holding mine. My only blurred hope was that the metal bit about to penetrate my skull was more hi-tech than that used for household do-it-yourself work.

The journey was an operation in itself. Because of my unstable neck fracture and the fear of further damage, the doctors collaborated with air-ambulance and police to find the smoothest, safest route possible from Scotland to England. I was flown from Aberdeen to Leeds-Bradford airport, and then escorted by a host of police, whilst laid regally in an ambulance. Potholes in the road had been circled in chalk ahead of us, and the police even closed the M1 motorway so that we could have the most bump-free journey possible. So much fuss for one person. Me. I felt overwhelmed by their kindness.

Later I woke, to a disturbed-looking brother recovering from his own drill-related trauma, and to a new design of neck-stabilizer. Its vertical black bars in my line of vision seemed horribly symbolic – my own prison cell encasing a restless soul now locked inside an almost useless assemblage of muscles and bones that masqueraded as my body.

My new home was far from the safe, protected, attentive environment of intensive care. The drugs stopped. My tears trickled throughout the night. Paralysis was suddenly very real. Life entered a new blur, this time induced by depression rather than by drugs. A whole new hoard of white coats came to visit, prodding me and asking questions. If I strained my eyes far enough sideways, I could just make out people in wheelchairs rolling by. The stark reality of my new situation struck painfully at my heart.

I detested mornings. I hated being woken by a new shift of nurses at an unsociably early hour – for what? To lie there, utterly bored with my view of more white ceiling tiles! To churn the concept of paralysis around my mind, trying to comprehend it with no inkling of how to begin. I would try to fool the nurses, and myself, that I was still sleeping, pulling the sheet up over my head, desperate to return to my dreamland.

I put on new climbing boots. Their virgin black rubber soles and suede-like turquoise uppers felt soft and cold against my skin. I squeeze my feet into their two-sizes-too-small fit. The luminous yellow and pink laces shout adventure at me. My excitement rises as I slip the harness over my hips, the metal climbing gear hanging from its loops, cold even through my leggings.

I inspect the rock, vanishing into the mist above. Three inexperienced, apprehensive, but very eager friends, we stand at the bottom of a classic route on the mountain of Tryfan in North Wales.

The rock is rough and harsh on the fingers. My hands are raw from the day before, the skin chafed and sore. The atmosphere feels electric as we search out the climb and match the guidebook to the mountain. Adrenaline feeds our appetite, encouraging us higher, immersing us deeper in cloud.

At the summit, we celebrate, each of us leaping the gap

Climbing on Tryfan, North Wales, Summer 1989

between the two trig points, called Adam and Eve, sharing our happiness at being safe and high. The mist is still swirling as we begin a murky descent of the path and our efforts are rewarded as slowly, sunlight burns away the gloom of the afternoon clouds.

The brightness was not the sun, but the glare of hospital strip lights permeating a glow through the starched sheets.

The nurses would arrive, frustratingly cheery, with a bowl of water and soap to give me a daily wash. The transition zone across my chest, where sensation went from full to zero in a few inches, was uncomfortably hypersensitive. When the cloth brushed over this part of my skin, I would flinch with the electrical tingling

Adam and Eve, stones at the summit of Tryfan, North Wales, summer 1989 Climbing with friend Helen Taylor (& Ruth Crossley, not in picture)

sensation of my confused nerves. I was jealous of the nurses who walked efficiently around the ward, tending to patients. I was envious that they could move. I watched their leg muscles as they walked to and from my bed. The reality and craziness of my new situation shocked me. The pain began to seep through the façade of drugs that had eased me into this new world. Reality was like a bizarre and sinister screensaver that I wished I knew how to change.

I spoke very little. I sank into a dark pool within, and only occasionally came out for a gasp of air and to speak to Mum, Dad or Simon. When I did, I was distraught. I was in deep water, couldn't find the bottom with my feet, and could only see the life that I'd known slipping away towards a distant horizon, daylight fading. What would I do if I couldn't run or climb again? How could I live without being in the mountains? The life that I'd known seemed so close and vivid, yet I couldn't touch it. How could I be a geologist if I couldn't walk? How could I do fieldwork? Would I be able to return to my postgraduate studies in Aberdeen? It was like looking through a giant windscreen, which once had a clear and beautiful view, now cracked so badly that I could only see a devastated scene. Everything that my life and my identity were built around felt shattered. I was tortured by dreams that I couldn't see how I'd ever bring to life.

There was nothing anyone could say or do to change or improve the situation. I knew that time, patience and my own mind were the only things that could heal. I kept my feelings hidden as best as I could, even when my mind was festering with depression, and worked things out for myself. I thought it would only hurt those I loved more if they knew how much I was hurting. I believed it would only re-enforce their feelings of helplessness if I revealed my thoughts. After the first week in the spinal unit, I mostly weathered my emotions alone. I refused to share the deep pain inside, and I think I refused to wholly experience it myself too. Of course, I wasn't conscious of that, or of the black hole within me. I did a great job of staying focused on 'task', just getting on with the practicalities of recovery. I had a few solid friendships that saw me through the difficult stuff, right the way through to today. But I experienced a deep loneliness even though people were around me. I felt that sharing too much would burden other people, and I didn't want to do that. I was blueprinted with this need to be strong and hold it all together, even when I felt like old stringy superglue that could barely do the job. I realize now that sometimes, sharing the deepest, darkest places within us with others is how life becomes richer, friendships stronger and relationships more meaningful. I experienced some of that to an extent, but not so deeply as I could have done if I hadn't been so unconsciously obsessed with putting on a brave face.

I closed my eyes and concentrated hard on wiggling my toes. I strained my imagination to the point that I was sure I could wiggle them just a little. I heard that if you regained any movement within the first few weeks after injury, then paralysis might only be temporary, caused by initial swelling and bruising of the spinal cord. Convinced there was some progress, I asked visitors to scrutinize my feet as I searched for the connection between my brain and my lower limbs. Sadly, they had to tell me there wasn't the slightest sign of movement.

My friend Will sat long hours at my bedside, talking and joking, telling funny stories of his travels in Nepal, where he had spent a summer shuttling exam papers between mountain villages. He told me a story about a small boy, seven or eight years old, who the villagers said was gifted. Will had watched the boy move a giant-sized boulder, impossible for any other fully-grown, muscle-endowed man to budge.

He left me pondering how such things were possible. He usually visited late, and as both my arms were still locked-up in plaster, he would help me clean my teeth, laughing at the cup and straw technique as I gargled and choked on toothpaste that gravitated to the back of my throat.

When I had no visitors, and no distraction, an oppressive silence engulfed me. I aimlessly watched the comings and goings of the hospital ward, filled with almost unbearable jealousy at the sight of people walking.

I felt a prisoner within my own body.

CHAPTER 3

LEARNING AGAIN

Be willing to accept the shadows
that walk across the sun
If this world were a perfect place
where would souls go to school
Do not weep for the limitations
that you see existing in your world
Those limitations are there for a purpose
Where would there be an opportunity to learn
If not in the world of imperfection?

Do not grieve for those who suffer,
who are subjected to limited capacities for living.
View your world as a transient place
where souls choose to come
because this is what they have selected
as their mode of learning
to the most minute detail.
EMMANUEL

Before I would be fit to return to the 'outside world', I apparently required at least a four-month apprenticeship. With my spinal cord severed, I could no longer transmit messages from my brain to the rest of my body. No movement, no sensation and no control of my bodily functions below chest level. The consultant had a no-nonsense way of letting me know exactly what this meant: "You have the control of a baby. You have to learn how to urinate again, how to move your bowels and how to look after yourself". That's exactly what the next months involved.

We, the 'inmates', were all there fighting our own challenges, and helping each other through them. There was an amazing openness – with a different nurse's hand up each of our backsides every few days, inserting suppositories and extracting the results, our pride and privacy were quickly destroyed. Everyone was 'in it together'. We lay in our rows of beds for days on end, staring at our patches of ceiling, each dreaming of the day when we could just get up. Like a rack of sausages on a barbecue we were turned every few hours to make sure our skin wasn't 'overdone' and we didn't get pressure sores.

My life became much more interesting with a mirror, strategically positioned at an angle above my head to reflect a glimpse of the world around me. Everything was upside down of course, but certainly more interesting than the ceiling. I could make out the underside-chin of the man opposite, and it was liberating to suddenly be able to match names and voices to chins or body shapes under the sheets. I'm still amazed at how I sustained so many hours and weeks of staring at a ceiling. I couldn't hold a book with my broken arms, or watch a television from my horizontal position. I had no entertainment other than talking to companions, friends and family. But that was enough. I think my mind was fighting so hard to cope with the shock of all that had happened, that I had no energy or interest left to wonder what was happening in the news, to read or be 'intellectual'. I thought a lot. And I did a lot of being 'brain dead'. When I thought, I questioned what had happened. I wondered what next. I conjectured over what might have been, how things could have been different. I wondered 'What if?' Strangely, I never felt angry for anything. I never visited blame. The rest of the time, I just stared at the ceiling, mentally 'knocked out', with all the brain power of a cabbage.

My fellow 'inmates' included Harvey, paralysed overnight by a flu injection. Chris, on bed rest, but fortunately not paralysed despite racing his motorbike into a wall of tyres at high speed. There was another guy who had been paralysed when thrown over the handlebars of a mountain bike he'd nicked, whilst making a getaway across a potholed field. The stories were endlessly varied – from the more common themes of rugby, motorbikes, horse-riding and diving into shallow swimming pools, to being shot in the spine or falling off a bar stool! There was also Frank, who for weeks had just been a mysterious rasping voice to me. Through the mirror I understood why I'd pictured him as an old man. He was young, but his voice was constrained and distorted by the ventilator on which he relied for air in order to speak. He was one of the unluckiest of us, paralysis affecting him from the neck down.

The mornings were always long and quiet, and conversation between the rows of ceiling-staring inmates was slow. We made no attempt to encourage each other to speak. Personal space was limited enough, and we all had an unspoken respect for each other's need for time to think. If we were feeling sociable, we might engage in trivial conversation about the unfolding day around us – the stunning hospital cuisine of cardboard toast, cold enough to harden butter, or the green-cotton-clad cleaners who came to mop the floors and attempted to cheer us up. Water jugs at our bedsides would be re-filled with dishwater-flavoured orange squash. A few physios would filter into the ward and, judging by the sound effects, induce pain and torture to their selected victims. Then quiet would descend for a while, before the lunchtime bustle started.

After two months of lying on my back in the hospital ward, brain numbed by my ceiling-tile view, staff volunteered to wheel our beds into the warm, sunny fresh air and I jumped at the chance. It was March since I'd last breathed fresh air, that Scottish Sunday morning, and now it was almost June. It was incredible to rediscover the world outside; to lie and see the rich colours of leaves, to listen to their soft whispers in the breeze, against a flawless blue sky. To hear birds, to smell cut grass, to feel the sun warm my face. I absorbed every detail, every subtle and delicate beauty of nature. As dusk fell and everyone else returned inside, I stayed, mesmerized by the night sky, stars glinting down at me as if they held all the answers to the questions that had buzzed in my head over the past weeks. Around midnight, when the cold finally started to penetrate the starched hospital sheets, I allowed myself to be wheeled back to my position in the row of beds in the ward.

We were shuffled around on a regular basis on the hospital ward, apparently to stop us from becoming 'institutionalised'. It was designed to keep us fresh, and I guess to alleviate any friction that might occur between bed neighbours should anyone find themselves next to someone they didn't get along with. It also meant though, that firm, long-lasting friendships were hard to form. We all had rigorous rehab schedules, from lifting weights, bouncing balls and learning to manage in a 'mock-up' kitchen, and were often tired or emotionally fragile. I remember all the faces and personalities that surrounded me in those months but I'm not in touch with any of them. I'm forever grateful for the companionship that we shared, but it was only the adversity of our calamities that we really had in common.

By early June, around ten weeks after my fall, the doctors deemed that my broken limbs and bones were healed. I had never had any surgery on my spine to stabilize its broken bones. The recommendation was simply to leave things to settle and heal, and then to work with whatever function I was left with after that. So the day had finally arrived when it was time to get up. I was excited but very apprehensive. I had adapted to life upside down in the mirror, and as the nurses lifted the back of my bed to introduce me to a sitting position, it was strange to see how everything looked when viewed the right way up.

Dizziness washed over me, and within a few minutes of being upright I had to return to my familiar, more comforting, horizontal position. It took a few more attempts before I finally progressed out of bed. Despite weeks of watching people passing by in wheelchairs, nothing could have prepared me for the alien feeling of being wheeled rather than walking.

It felt horrific. I felt exceedingly awkward. My confidence had been smashed out of me. The physically able, athletic body that I remembered had changed beyond recognition. My stomach muscles, relaxed and unable to work, left me with a pot-belly that I was disproportionately self-conscious of. The flesh and useless muscle seemed to hang from the bones of my legs with all the tone of deflated old balloons. I rushed back to bed soon after getting up for fear that someone I knew might arrive and catch me sitting in the wheelchair. I didn't want to be associated with such an ugly contraption; its steel frame and burgundy leather upholstery reeked of disability. By visiting time in mid-afternoon, I was always safely back in my bed, wheelchair cast to the side, my association with it a secret, shared only with the others who lived on the ward. How is it that I could be so embarrassed by circumstances that life had presented me with? I guess anything that batters our self-image, punches our confidence, changes our self-identity and challenges our ego in some way can have that affect. I'd certainly lost all reference to who I thought I was.

With daily physiotherapy I began to re-build my upper body strength. It took me two weeks to learn to sit up now that I had no control over my stomach muscles, but I soon progressed to more advanced moves. I could now transfer myself from the wheelchair to my bed, a toilet, a car – and the ultimate achievement – a bath! Moving from the bath to my chair required a certain degree of arm strength and balance, both of which needed perfecting. I pushed myself up out of the bath and hovered in the air briefly, trying to swing my bum to the side. Just when I thought I'd mastered the move, my hand slipped and I crashed back into the water, a tidal wave bursting over the bath sides and flooding the room. All this was performed under the instruction of a dedicated physio. Any dignity and self-consciousness was lost whilst I was 'trained in transfers' with my lifeless naked body attempting to negotiate even the simplest daily tasks.

I felt a little guilty when I compared my progress with that of some of the more severely injured friends around me. Harvey was still lying on his back due to the complication of a pressure sore, and Frank's challenges were different – having to learn to maximize the speech he gained from each breath.

We were all trying to learn new skills for living in our own ways; whether this was dealing with the need to pee through a tube and the daily chore of catheters, coping with the need to encourage one's colon with a rubber-gloved hand, or just re-learning how to breathe. I am amazed at the strength that we all found within ourselves to cope with our scary new worlds. With our physical identities threatened so harshly, we all found an inner strength, derived from a need to get back to our homes, our families and some 'normality' of environment. Getting back to our lives as quickly as possible was a major motivator.

In many ways it was like being a child again. I could entertain myself for hours exploring and discovering all the new things I needed to grasp – the new workings of my body, or how to manipulate a wheelchair without flipping it backwards or catapulting myself onto the floor. The hospital and its grounds were my new playground and I spent hours learning the smallest of new skills. Jumping my wheelchair up a kerb and doing wheelies down a ramp were the moves I was most determined to master. I kept getting myself in troublesome situations, like the evening I fell out of my wheelchair whilst doing laps around the hospital grounds. I called to a passer-by to help me and it turned out he was completely blind. What a team! Like a two-year old in a sandpit, as long as I was learning, I was entertained, and distracted from my feelings of devastation.

Life in the spinal unit was intense. It was distressing and frustrating, but there were other times when I wept with laughter.

It never ceased to be interesting and challenging, but nothing could fully prepare me for re-joining the world outside. The unit was a cocoon – people around me knew the issues, understood the enormity and entirety of what we were all facing and empathized a little. Being paralysed was the norm. Outside I was an anomaly.

CHAPTER 4

FEELING THE PAIN

"There is no coming to consciousness without pain."
C.G. JUNG

I'd begun to have weekends away from the hospital, slowly adapting to joining the outside world full time. Most of these weekends I spent with my parents at our family home in Yorkshire, and a few close friends would come to spend time with me, helping me mentally adapt and begin to explore what I could do in this new 'zone', a million miles from my old comfort zone.

My blueprint of trying to be strong and keeping it together persisted with a force. I didn't want to add fuel to the fire of pain that roared around me, so I stubbornly put on a brave face, a smile, and pretended that it was all okay and that I could take it in my stride. But in truth I was thrown into the chasms of my psyche and into shadows that I'd rather not have confronted – I felt fear, jealousy, sadness and loneliness. The pain of loss seared through me so deeply that recalling memories of life before the fall felt like being stabbed in the heart. Everything was the same, yet nothing seemed the same. Memories hurt most, and the only way I could avoid my memories was to keep myself very, very busy. I never stopped. I never allowed myself to be still, as I was scared of the intensity of the pain that might envelop me. My only reprieve from the night-mare was, consciously or unconsciously, distraction and avoidance.

So I kept busy, and tried to find fun in discov-ering what I could do. I'm lucky that I'm inherently an optimist. Although it was hard, and I got sad and weepy a great deal, there was this part within me that just kept getting back up again each time I slipped down. I think we all have that ability in us, but per-

Walking to the climb, Hornli Ridge, Matterhorn, Switzerland, August 1991

haps it's a fine line between managing to find the optimism and losing our way. The support we get in difficult times can be enough to tip that balance, and I was lucky to have the family, friends and environment that somehow nurtured my ability to stay positive. If I'd been surrounded by people saying "Poor you, how terrible, what are you ever going to do now?" then I'm sure I wouldn't have been able to find the optimist within me. But as it was, I had friends saying "Come on, let's go back to the hills" or "So when are you going to start back in Aberdeen?" It drove me forwards but didn't stop me from taking small steps backwards when I needed to.

I was grieving, for the loss of my life and myself as I had known me. I read about grief and the 'grief process' and understood that we are supposed to go through stages of shock and denial where we fluctuate between painful reality and distraction, then disorganization with the intense emotion and chaos of adjusting, and finally acceptance where the intensity of pain recedes and balance and quality of life is found again. I couldn't recognize or accept that I was immersed in that cycle, nor did it actually matter. The theory was, frankly, not remotely helpful when the hard facts of my new reality faced me every day. I had taken freedom for granted. Paralysis forced me to appreciate what freedom meant to me – freedom of movement, freedom of expression, freedom to walk anywhere – along the banks of a river, through a woodland, up a hill, across a field.

I'd never even considered movement as a form of freedom. I'd never considered its importance to me until it was taken away. I became absorbed in fascination with movement. I felt overwhelmed with awe and envy just watching people move. The simplest things were the most jealousy provoking – standing up, climbing a few steps, bending over, crossing legs – all actions that had once seemed so simple, such everyday, ordinary, taken-for-granted things now seemed so very incredible. I sat in the same chair, in the same position, and felt unable to express myself. I wanted to jump up and down with excitement, to run into virgin snow and roll in it and fool around. I wanted to be able to hug someone close without feeling awkwardness.

I discovered a need for anything that allowed a different body position, or an alternative way of moving the parts of me that I still could. I would slide from my wheelchair and lie on the floor – on my back, front, side – and stretch, bend and move my legs with my arms. Even this, trivial though it may seem, made me feel just a tiny bit more free.

I imagined not even having the use of my arms, just like Frank and the others I'd known in the spinal unit. I couldn't comprehend how anyone's mind could cope with the massive removal of movement that paralysis from the neck down would bring. At least paraplegia allowed me the freedom to dress myself, go for a walk alone, hold a book, scratch an itch and hug someone. If the break in my neck had been slightly more serious then my freedom to speak would have been taken away too.

I spent long days, alone, contemplating all of this. I wondered what I could make of my new circumstances. I thought about freedom. I read a book, *The Diving Bell & The Butterfly*, about a man who is completely paralysed, is speechless and only able to move one eyelid, yet still manages to find the courage and energy to write a book – dictated through movements of his eyelid. I wondered at the capacity of the mind to adjust and adapt to any situation, given time and the will. Maybe the gift of a mind is the only freedom we need. At least I still had a mind that seemed to be in good working order.

I needed no greater reminder of how fortunate I was than the company of my fellow 'inmates'. If I was feeling sorry for myself because I couldn't climb mountains anymore, another inmate might cry out with joy and achievement at finally managing to utilise their limited hand function to peel a banana on their own. If I was feeling grateful that my friend Will had cleaned my teeth for me again, knowing that soon my broken arms would be healed and I could do it myself, then I might turn my head sideways and see my neighbour Frank, unable to speak without a ventilator and with no prospects of ever being able to move his arms again. If I was feeling proud that I had managed to dress myself, an inmate might say goodbye, their spinal injury having fully repaired, allowing them to walk out of the hospital and home to a relatively 'normal' life. The hospital ward in which I had lain for so many months provided a microcosm of the disparity in the world.

We can all find somebody worse off than ourselves, and comparing myself to those around me was sometimes very effective. Remembering good reasons not to feel so sorry for myself could give me a required kick-up-the-backside. Our personal traumas and challenges can easily fade into insignificance when compared to the bigger picture of the world and the tragedies that occur within it. Most days, however, comparison was a futile, pointless activity. I had what I had, and I knew that others all over the world were richer or poorer in the different senses of those words.

I was forced to think deeply about what had led me to this place. I hadn't been driven by a need to compete and accumulate trophies, awards and material possessions, but by my desire to climb increasingly difficult routes, reach the summit of higher mountains and achieve what I perceived to be more and more physically impressive feats. Who had I been trying to impress? Myself or others? What had I been trying to prove?

I had been pushed by my ego to climb higher, harder and better. I had been living in my head and ignoring my heart. Every cell in my body had been screaming with fear just minutes before my accident, in the very first part of the climb. They had been screaming at me to take notice, to get out of there whilst I still could. They had been warning me. Yet I had pushed on, ignoring the nervous flutter in my heart, dismissing the shaking cells of my body, determined to climb...and to fall.

I had been so busy striving that I'd pushed myself and my luck to the limits – it wasn't, in retrospect, a surprise that I'd ended up paralysed. I was lucky to be alive. If I hadn't been so headstrong but listened to the subtler messages of my heart, which had pleaded with me on that cliff face and on many of my previous adventures, "Go down! It's too hard!" then I probably wouldn't have splattered myself at the cliff base that day.

I found my accident futile and pointless. It seemed like a terrible waste and all I could see were my hopes and dreams washing away like water down life's plughole. My sense of loss accompanied me everywhere. There was no moment of the day and no situation where I could escape the imprisonment that I experienced within my lifeless body. How could I find purpose and meaning in all of this trauma?

Various sympathetic souls gave me books to read and tapes to listen to with stories that I suppose they hoped I would find inspirational. One was the story of how Joni, paralysed from the neck down in a diving accident, had found Christianity and become a great artist, painting with her mouth. I'm sure if Christopher Reeve had been injured at this point, I would have been showered with motivational stories of 'Superman', his dedication to physio-therapy, and his ability to move his toe again. But at that moment, none of it made any sense to me.

I got talking to a lady in a cafe. She had just lost her husband. As I sat listening to her describe her loss, I could relate to it exactly. Losing my movement was losing the life I had known.

Losing a close loved one had a similar impact – the life she'd known, the person she'd loved and trusted was gone. The body I knew was also gone. We'd both had to learn all over again. We'd both been thrown completely outside our comfort zones, forced into situations we'd rather not be in. Everything was different and the world suddenly seemed an alien, scary place. For different reasons, we both felt very alone.

I knew friends had tried to understand and empathize with my paralysis, but I believed that nobody could really know what my loss meant to me. I thought it was too personal and something that I just had to cope with on my own. I had taken it on as my own personal battle, to overcome my fears and face the new challenges. In lots of ways this was true, but I realized in that conversation, that I wasn't really alone.

My striving to achieve in the physical sense had been driven by something within me that placed value on physical excellence. Other people strive to achieve in other ways like through their career, status or in monetary terms. It dawned on me that striving in these ways, and building self-identity around it is a very fragile thing. One unexpected event could shatter the illusion, and it had for me. I felt humbled, vulnerable and human. That was a good thing I'm sure, but I wished very hard that I'd been able to hear the quiet voice inside me, and stopped my striving madness before it had stopped me.

We all face challenges throughout life, in so many shapes and sizes, whether its physical injury, coping with death, stress, depression, illness, burn-out, redundancy...the list of possible challenges that might erupt before us is endless. We are all confronted with the raw emotions of fear and loneliness in a multitude of forms. They can strike us anytime, anywhere, anyhow, and often seem unfair, random, unjust and certainly unexpected. Our circumstances are hauled into chaos and instability, leaving us threatened with fear and uncertainty, and catapulted way out of our comfort zone. We are forced to face our new circumstances, and perhaps pushed into looking at our life or ourselves in a new way. It is scary, hard and shocking when 'shit' happens to us, when we almost believed we were immune. I wondered if my accident would have been preventable if I'd filtered my actions through listening to my heart and my intuition. Probably I wouldn't have got myself into the scary position on that cliff that I had. How many of the challenges that confront us in life are preventable in this way?

For months I had been wondering how to overcome the engulfing loss, the sense of drowning in sadness that followed me. I'd wondered how to shake off the loneliness, and the feeling of isolation and disconnection with the people and places around me. I'd believed that no-one could understand my loss or relate to it. But now I realized that my emotions weren't all that unusual. It somehow offered me a shaft of light in knowing that I didn't need to think of myself as quite so alone anymore.

Through my weekends at home I was becoming more engaged with the world outside. I'd begun talking to the University and to friends in Aberdeen about when to move back there and continue with my studies. The University offered me a postgraduate grant to support me for three years, and an accessible flat in a hall of residence. I jumped at the chance of reintroducing a part of my 'old' life: it seemed the only sensible way to introduce a thread of normality. I began to plan the best part of a week away from the hospital, so that I could travel up to Scotland and begin to set things up for returning. After visiting the University and making arrangements there, a plan evolved to spend the weekend with Aberdeen friends on a visit to the Orkney Isles. I craved anything outside the hospital, but I felt a mix of excitement and fear as Dad drove me north.

We sorted out the practical arrangements for returning to study, and then, with the very large heavy wheelchair, I joined Pete, Isla, and a few other friends and we squashed into Pete's slowly rusting car, destined for John O'Groats and a ferry to the Orkney Isles. I was looking forward to seeing the hills and mountains of the Island of Hoy. It was famous for 'The Old Man', a sea stack visited by many climbers. I longed to admire its rock walls rising a few hundred metres from the foam and the spray that licks at its base.

I rolled around the boat in time with the rhythmic swell of the sea. It was a rough crossing, with black storms brewing over the Pentland Firth. As we arrived, the rain blew in sheets across the white-capped waves. It was a dark, unwelcoming arrival and we quickly hid ourselves in a cozy Stromness pub. We'd planned to camp, but with the lashing weather, we ended up sleeping in the 'Italian Chapel' on giant airbeds beneath the altar. It was a bizarre and amusing experience, distinct from the routine sterility of hospital, especially when we had to pack and leave in a hurry the next morning as tourist vans started arriving at early doors.

The following day we left the Hoy ferry port, and the others went ahead in the car to search for a bothy we knew existed on the other side of the island. It was only a few miles by road, and I decided to push myself there.

The single-track, sheep-lined lane climbed through the hills, their rough texture a vivid contrast to the cultivated fields of the main island. Unexpected emotion flooded through me. It was the first time I'd seen mountains again. They were just molehills really, but silent and solid and with all the majesty of those much higher. My senses were shaken. Their colours, once just shades of brown and green, were vivid and bright to me now. Their streams were musical, twisting and bubbling a rocky pathway downwards. The sky was grey and once this would have seemed an unspectacular day – just a road across some insignificant hills. Today it was different – it was the world I had been dreaming of. It was a world I had been deprived of for months. Everything looked sharper, the colours richer, and the sounds louder.

But it was painful. Mountains and wilderness had always offered me peace and calm. But now they created conflict. I felt honoured and privileged to be there, yet torn apart with a blast of emotions.

The bothy sat in a wide bay, a bank of smooth boulders climbing up from the shore to its door. High cliffs rose steeply on either side of the beach, backed by grassy slopes leading up to the hills. It was a beautiful spot. I sat amongst the boulders of the storm-washed beach, where my friends had carried me, and I felt like a stunned animal caught in bright headlights, unsure of whether to run or stay.

I lay on the floor of the bothy in my sleeping bag, hugging myself in an attempt to keep warm. The smell of wood-smoke filled my lungs. The cold penetrated from the flagstone floor, the crackling logs too distant to offer warmth. The window silhouetted an old tin kettle, and the heather thatch bulged from above. Outside the wind whisked the Pentland Firth, crashing surf against rainbow cliffs. Most of the others were walking to 'The Old Man', probably shrouded in cloud. I imagined a brisk fresh walk, being blown drunkenly around the cliff tops, the sensation of rain lashing against my face. I lay still on the hard cold floor.

The icy flags somehow cut to the pain of my loss. A storm like the one that battered outside boiled through me.

We were only on the island for three days, but I was glad to return to Aberdeen. The city tormented me less.

I continued to make more trips to the mountains but the emotions they stirred were very raw.

It wondered if it might be easier not to visit these places any more. If I didn't see mountains, maybe I could forget them. Maybe it would be better to remember places as I used to, and to start again in a world without hills, in a land of concrete and tarmac.

But gradually I realized that I had no choice. Mountains and wilderness were too much a part of me. I had to find a way to access that again. I wanted to feel close again to the beauty and freedom of rugged, natural places. The emotions they stirred were painful, but something forced me to keep going back.

I just couldn't abandon all of this to my memories. But how could I find the courage to go forward?

CHAPTER 5

THE UNCERTAINTY OF LIFE

"Even after the heaviest storm the birds come out singing, so why can't we delight in whatever good thing remains to us?"
'Even After the Heaviest Storm', ROSE KENNEDY

After the fall, I thought a lot about climbing. The highlight was being surrounded by mountains. Feeling their vastness and majesty put into perspective the trivialities of daily life, which might otherwise become all consuming. I never believed I was immortal, but prior to the fall, I never took the possibility of death or injury seriously. I knew the risks involved, but I never really considered them. Maybe I didn't quite appreciate the value of life at that point. I took being physically healthy, able and active for granted. Anything less seemed something far away, reserved for old age, or very bad luck. Whilst climbing I felt invincible.

Even if I'd considered the risk, I'm sure I'd have carried on doing what I did. I would have reasoned that I could get run over by a bus tomorrow, so why hold back on life? With hindsight, I believe it's not about avoiding the risk, but about being aware enough to know when to proceed with an endeavor, and when not to.

Climbing with Will Ramsbotham, Eldorado, Switzerland, August 1992 (climb led by Al Powell)

Before Will had become my evening teeth-cleaning buddy and storyteller, we had run and climbed together often, sharing our passion for the outdoors. He had a child-like excitement about him, always a bouncing and colourful bundle of energy. I often remember one particular climb that we did together. It was a spectacular Swiss rock face, with towering slabs devoid of cracks or holes that disappeared high into the clear Alpine sky.

We had climbed as a three, and Will and I had shouted encouragement and praise to our bolder partner, Al, when he negotiated a difficult move. Most of the time, Al sweating and working hard above us, we stared out at the stunning vista from whichever ledge we happened to be nestled on at the time, reliably blue summer sky presiding over a mass of summits. We joked, laughed, and ate a mini-mountain of peanuts and raisins, leaving a trail of them spilled on ledges as we climbed towards the sky.

It was one of those special days one never forgets.

It was also the last time we climbed together.

Climbing and other adventure sports are not just about adrenaline. So much of the enjoyment is about the strength of friendships formed. Climbing partners develop a camaraderie and depth of feeling through sharing their task and life on a rope. The visions climbers share from mountain ledges somehow bridge any gaps in daily life. It was that strength of friendship that led Will to make regular cycling outings from his home in Leeds to the hospital in Wakefield. His cycle trips were generous excuses to see a climbing partner through difficult times whilst feeding his need to exercise. Perhaps they were also a space to consider his uncertainty about the risks of the sport we both loved.

Occasionally he would come in his rusty Astra instead of the bike. On a couple of these visits, we sheltered from the rain under an overhanging part of the hospital, sanding and painting the patches of rust on his car. It might have seemed a very dull thing to do, except it felt like the most exciting, normal and useful thing I'd done in months. Nothing was ever said, but I knew that he'd designed the activity for that reason.

After long hours chatting in hospital, I knew Will had thought a lot about whether to continue climbing. His love of the mountains made him, in part, the person he was. I never discouraged any of my friends from continuing to climb, but for a few months Will shied away from scaling rock faces.

He visited me in hospital one evening and told me of his plans to go to North Wales that weekend. He talked of the house where his family lived; his love for them and his home effused from him. He mentioned Cader Idris, his favourite mountain, and I had an inkling that he would be climbing there that weekend. I didn't want to ask, and he artfully avoided the topic for my sake. However, I could see that the allure of being part of the giant rock playground again was sorely tempting.

It was the last time Will climbed. He died that June weekend. A nurse came to my bedside to pass on the news.

I was numb. A roar of emotion flooded through me, disabling any chance of a rational, larger perspective. I was caught in a whirlwind of loss; Will's death tying the chains of grief more tightly around me than ever. How could life have been snatched away so viciously? He was so young and bursting with energy, dreams, love and compassion. Why had he been unfairly taken from life when he had so much to give and so far to go? The terrible feeling of loss embedded itself deep within me, and in all who knew him.

The story of Will's death unfolded. He and his friend had reached the summit of Cader Idris after a great day on the mountain. They descended by abseil, but on the way down the rope got tangled and Will paused to unravel it. Whilst shaking the rope, its anchor dislodged and when he put his weight back onto it, he plummeted hundreds of metres. Will was a scrupulously careful climber, but this wasn't enough to save him.

His void was blacker than mine.

The details didn't matter.

"Why him? Why not me?" Will's death pushed my emotions to another extreme. Long and hard I thought about him, about climbing, about life and death. Everyone walks such a fine tightrope. The human body, so resilient yet so vulnerable. You could live for decades and yet one wrong move and life could evaporate in an instant, the future vaporised into nothing.

The uncertainty of life startled me, and I savored my

memories as if they could erase all the loss that I felt. I wished that I'd appreciated every moment of each experience more fully.

A group of friends from Leeds, all fell-runners, left the chapel an hour before the funeral on a pilgrimage run. I pushed around the grounds, smelling the fresh cut grass that hinted of the approaching summer. Everyone who had known Will was richer for the experience. They were all gathered in the cold chapel when I wheeled, feeling horribly conspicuous, towards the front row. The coldness seeped deeper as I sat, tears pouring freely, listening to stories of Will and his smiling, infectious goodness.

I searched for things that Will had sent me and collected them preciously together. His letters had always cheered me up, his eloquent descriptions and entertaining detail about simple things; a view from a window, the dew on opening buds of flowers, colourful descriptions of people. He had a special ability to share pleasure from the smallest of things in life, a quality I admired. Whenever he had visited me, he thoughtfully never mentioned any of his activities, cautious not to stir memories of things I could no longer do.

I stared at a painting he had sent me with its bold title, 'The Yorkshire Daily Rag', running my fingers across the bumpy surface of the watercolour paper as if it would somehow bring him back to life. The painting was a spoof of the first evening I had got away from the spinal unit. Will had arrived in his now not-rusty Astra, into which I had performed a pathetic transfer, my chair shooting away from the car, planting my bottom on the tarmac. His script described the events of the evening – Scoop! A Ghoulie Moved My Chair! There was an artistic sketch of the scene and various watercolours liberally applied to highlight the image of me sprawled on the ground of the hospital car park.

Where had he gone? Was it really right to be sad for him? Maybe he was in a paradise land, far beyond the reach of my imagination. Maybe I should have been rejoicing for him, not wallowing in despair at his absence. Had his soul transcended to another world, or another dimension of this world? Or was he just dead, gone, to nothingness?

Every one of us, especially when faced with death, must ponder these questions. Where do we all come from? What are we doing here? Is there a purpose to living? Where, if anywhere, do we go when we depart from this world? Is there more to it? Could our existence really be as menial as just that... we exist, and then we are no more? Not surprisingly, I found no answers to these questions that have entertained the minds of great philosophers. But asking them and meeting the unknown of our world felt vitally important.

Stark and dear memories haunted me, and I couldn't cast from my heart the pain of all the loss and the loneliness I felt within. But what had happened had passed, and there was nothing I could do to change any of it. Bizarrely perhaps, I felt no anger or blame. None of this was anyone's fault. It was just how it was.

Something about Will's death pulled my attention away from feeling powerless in my new circumstances, to looking at what I could do, and how I could make the most of the new situation, rather than dwelling on a past that was no more. I felt presented with a very clear choice. I could choose whether to immerse myself in all the memories, and to focus on all the loss and sadness of it all, or I could concentrate on dealing with and making the most of my new circumstances.

And what choice did I have really? Did I want to spend my life feeling sad, living with these memories that I had no chance of re-living, or did I want to move on, jump into this new world I found myself immersed in, and see where its torrents would take me?

A few weeks previously, I'd woken up early with this deep but crazy feeling that becoming paralysed was a good thing to have happened to me. How crazy was that? Except there were no hallucinogenic painkillers involved any more, and I was never more sober or feeling more in touch with reality. I had shared with a friend this strange revelation, that perhaps my new circumstances weren't such a bad thing after all. I had this intense feeling that being paralysed would enable me to learn valuable things, show me things that I'd otherwise have been blind to, teach me about myself and the world. My brain told me that it was an absolutely disastrous thing to have happened. How could there be anything good about being paralysed? But as I gained some distance from the rawness of my accident, I began to feel less and less that it was senseless and unfair. I was able to reflect on the suffering I was experiencing, and to think about what it might mean. Something about Will dying forced me to find a new strength derived from a sense that my surviving had purpose.

It seemed that somewhere deep within me was a glimmer on the sea of despair. I wanted to discover the meaning in my life and my experience.

Did this feeling stem from some kind of survival instinct, screaming at me to see positive perspectives and leave the dungeons of my mind, or was it an intuitive and spiritual moment... a voice from within or above? It didn't matter. The fact was, somewhere deep within me was a craving to find the positive in my new situation, and Will's death had the effect of adding fuel to this tiny flame.

One minute we can be coasting along in life, and the next we're standing in a raging storm wondering what happened. My own accident, and Will's death, left me and so many others standing in a giant puddle with the torrents of tragedy pouring onto our heads. But what Will's misfortune did for me was to wake me up. Sometimes it takes a person or an event to awaken in us the resources that we need to grab a challenge or difficulty we are experiencing by the horns, and fight it.

Life became suddenly precious. How could I ever have been foolish enough to think I'd rather be dead than paralysed? For some reason, I was still alive, privileged enough to have the chance to engage with life, to realize dreams, to experience love. I was filled with a new determination to make the most of everything I still had, and a new purpose grew within me.

With a sense of urgency, I threw myself into life and activity. The tragedy of Will's death had made me value life and gave me the courage to engage with it wholeheartedly again.

CHAPTER 6

A MASKED FRENZY

*"There is only one courage, and that is the courage to go
on dying to the past. Not to collect it, not to accumulate
it, not to cling to it. We all cling to the past, and because
we cling to it we become unavailable to the present."*
BHAGWAN SHREE RAJNEESH

Only a few months ago, I had laid in a hospital bed, struggling
to imagine how I would ever learn to sit-up again, without
the use of my abdominal muscles. I recalled lying on my side,
feeling swallowed by the plastic-coated mattress and starched
sheets, watching wheelchair athletes on the TV, speeding their way
through the London Marathon. I was inspired on one level, yet on
another I felt helpless and useless, wondering how on earth I could
possibly get from my current state of mind and health to achieving
something so physically demanding. "How do they do it? How can
I ever do that? How?" Their achievements impressed me, and a
small, subconscious part of me decided that I would like to push
myself around a marathon too. Yet a greater part of me wondered
how I could ever manage it.

The last time I had run a race was with Will. It was a
cross-country relay in a forest just outside Aberdeen. It was only a

few months now before I would return to Scotland, and I decided that doing a race in my wheelchair would be a good start to building my strength and being more physically active again. I would shortly be tackling the challenge of driving a car with hand controls (which incidentally left me wishing I was an octopus, but eventually became second-nature) but for now, my friend Susan and I bundled into her car and drove to Wales with the aim of doing a half-marathon.

The Lake Vyrnwy half-marathon had an uphill start before following the shore around the perimeter of the lake. There was one other wheelchair racer, but he had a fancy racing chair with three wheels, so I only saw the back of him for a few seconds at the start line. I was pushing in my regular wheelchair, although it was lighter than the tank I had been supplied with in hospital.

The start area was busy with people stretching and jumping around in lycra and fleece. The smell of muscle rub drifted on the still air, and I tried to ignore my envy of the rippling physiques that jogged past me. Even though I was clearly in a 'running' class of my own, and knew that competition wasn't on the agenda, I felt butterflies in my stomach. As the flutters intensified, I realized that I was in a competition after all – with myself. My nervousness was just a symptom of the challenge I had set, and I knew I would be very disappointed if I didn't finish the course in what I considered to be a reasonable time.

The start gun cracked into the warm autumn air, and by the time I reached the top of the half-mile incline to the edge of the lake, there were already no runners left in sight. I pushed a solitary loop around the lake's shore. There was none of the atmosphere of races that I recalled, with bodies battling and oozing sweat. Within four miles, I glimpsed a small pack of lithe runners, already on the opposite side of the water, effortlessly sprinting the return stretch.

In what seemed like hours later, I reached the halfway drinks station. The plastic cups and water containers were being packed into the back of the 'sweep' van, as it journeyed around the course, collecting markers and redundant marshals. I found a few dregs of orange juice to recover some strength. I began again, settling into a rhythm, pushing the cold metal of my wheels whilst admiring the mountains and their mirrored reflection in the lake. I was resigned to the fact that I was last, but so happy just to be out there, living and breathing fresh air.

I missed feeling part of the event, but in a curious way I enjoyed being on my own, especially after all the months of being cooped up with constant company in the hospital. In the silence, broken only by the sound of my hands on the pushrims of the chair, I began to find myself again.

Finally I was zipping downhill towards the end, although the finishing posts were long-removed. To my surprise, I trundled past a woman staggering down the final hill, and I wasn't quite last to finish after all.

Despite it being very hard work, and although my wheelchair had rattled on the bumpy tarmac like a shopping trolley in gravel, I had really enjoyed the whole racing experience. I had missed these sensations – the physical exertion, feeling hot and red in the face, listening to my breath cutting the silence of the forest and enjoying the immersion in activity.

I enjoyed a long summer, in and out of hospital, with friends and with my family. They all supported me; physically, emotionally, practically and financially, as my PhD grant had long stopped. I felt fortunate to have the luxury of time, at least until September, before a normal routine and the need to engage my brain and get back into academia called. There were endless walks around the reservoirs of Yorkshire and Lancashire, discovering places with accessible paths or quiet lanes, preferably without kissing gates or cattle grids. People I hadn't previously thought of as close friends, became firm companions, and vice versa. Some of this making and withering of friendships was dictated by proximity and work circumstances, but some of it I'm sure was dictated by their ability to adjust to being with a friend they used to run or climb with, and not quite knowing what to say or how to be. Some people have an ability to adjust, to empathize and to connect more easily with the difficult stuff in life, and those are the people that became closer to me. Others find it uncomfortable, or maybe the only connection I had with them was one of shared activity, which it was now not possible to enjoy together in the same way.

At the end of the summer, six months after my fall, I moved back to Aberdeen. I'm sure it was a big day and a major milestone, but I don't remember much about it. Maybe something that helped me through the challenge of paralysis is that I'm quite a 'get-on-with-it' sort of person and I generally tend not to make a big fuss of occasions. So somehow, I found myself in a student flat, with an adequate grant to support me for three years, and a lifestyle that was self-managed and afforded me flexibility, as long as I progressed the 'rock research' I would be doing. I could earn a little extra by doing some student supervision work for under-graduates at the university. I felt I'd landed on a fortunate set of circumstances to ease me back into routine and life outside the hospital.

Adjusting emotionally involved an absolute immersion in physical activity. I would train twice a day, at the gym, learning to swim again, and gradually discovering more and more things that I could do. I find it exhausting just to remember and to write about, but it was almost certainly my way of coping and of trying to rebuild some of the identity I had lost. If I felt physically strong and capable, then I felt better about myself. Some of my activity frenzy was certainly about avoidance and denial, though I had no idea of that at the time. I've never stopped being an exercise-addict, but I have a more balanced, or at least less frantic, approach to it now than I did then.

After my experience in Wales, I was fortunate enough to be able to buy myself a racing wheelchair, thanks to some money that friends had raised to help me on the costly ladder of getting mobile. I began to train. The first few times I went to Aberdeen beach, and clumsily tried to push this strange racing machine into the winds blasting from the North Sea. I found it difficult, rapidly got sore muscles, and questioned why I had spent so much money on something that was *such* hard work. Yet I had made the decision to find a new way to be active, to get fit again, to lose all the weight I had gained in months of being static, obligingly munching the constant supply of chocolate and grapes brought by visitors, and to give myself a physical challenge.

I launched myself into training, unconsciously motivated by those images that still flickered in the archives of my mind, of the wheelchair athletes racing the London Marathon. In time, I began to enjoy the icy North Sea winds, especially when they blew from behind and propelled me quickly along the beach promenade as I dodged pets, kiddies and their strolling owners.

A year or so later, and some regular training under my belt, I was hooked. I joined a training week for wheelchair athletes at Stoke Mandeville and although it was fun, I mostly got dropped off the back of a pack of racers as we tore around the country lanes. But at the end of the week, I was offered a last-minute entry in the very race that I thought it would be years before I could consider doing - the London Marathon.

I was surprised to find myself there, on a busy, somewhat tense start line with a crowd of serious wheelchair athletes. Those images from the television as I'd lain in a hospital bed flashed back. I could hardly believe it! It was unexpected, unplanned, and very surprising to find myself in the race that only a year or so before I'd been astounded at the thought of. I felt proud, nervous, excited, and filled with a confidence and energy that I'd almost forgotten.

Loudspeakers babbled excitedly and camera-laden choppers buzzed overhead. I felt intimidated by the array of bright colours, flashy race-chairs and bulging shoulder muscles surrounding me. Serious faces hid beneath the shade of cycling helmets, already focused on the miles that lay ahead. I felt like an impostor, casually turning up at a few days notice and not really caring what position I achieved. I would just be happy to finish. There are so few wheelchair racers in the world compared to regular runners, that I was on the start line with the elite Paralympic athletes rather than amongst the crowds behind them. When the start gun sounded a train of impressive triangular physiques in their slick racing machines sped fast into the distance, and again, I found myself towards the back of the pack at a more sedate pace.

The atmosphere was fantastic. Giant speakers filled the streets, blasting reggae and beats to which I could time my pushing. A brass band piped up when it saw me approaching and it felt like the whole show was just for me – by now there were no other wheelchair racers in sight. The pantomime horses, giant hippos and three-legged runners that mark the mass of London marathon participants hadn't even started yet as we'd been first off. A television van came flying by then sat in front of me. I thought its crew were training their cameras on me, but they soon disappeared when a fast, black runner sprinted past, chased by the pack of elite men.

I soaked up the energy and cheers of the crowds, and pushed steadily through the twenty-six miles. To my amazement, the first twenty-two whizzed by, my attention focused on the sensation and amazement of taking part, but then I hit the quaint old cobbles of the Tower of London.

A red carpet had been laid across them to reduce the crippling effect of the bumpy stones on wheels and ankles. But as I strained up the uneven surface of the hill, the carpet soaked my energy like a sponge and the speedometer read zero miles per hour. For a moment I thought I would roll backwards. I was delirious for the last few miles. My brother Simon leapt out from the crowd and cheered encouragement at me, but I was so incoherent that I didn't even recognize him.

Just as I thought my arms would take me no further, the finishing straight finally arrived and with a last wave of effort, I completed my first marathon, exhausted and elated. The pain ended but my adrenaline still buzzed as I watched a crowd of silver foil runners stagger through the finishing funnels. Many of them looked in desperate need of a loan of my wheelchair! It felt a momentous occasion, and a long way to have come from watching the race on a screen in the hospital ward, whilst lying tied and trussed, unable to imagine even simple movement. I hugged Mum, Dad and Simon and was grateful that they were there to share the moment, especially at such short notice. Proud but weary I traveled home to Scotland with my medal hung around my neck.

The race-chair filled a certain niche, but it didn't give me the escape from the world of tarmac that I longed for. I still searched for other activities that would take me closer to nature, and I felt tired and sad inside at the constant effort it took. I'd left hospital to move back to Aberdeen and continue my studies in geology. I tried hard to put on a brave face and continue making an effort to go out, to get fit, to socialize – to live. Each evening in my small apartment I would sink into my sadness, go to bed early, and cry myself to sleep. In the morning as the daylight filtered through my thin blue curtains, I would long for it not to be morning, wishing I could sink back into the cushion of sleep rather than greet another day wearing a mask. Will's death may have given me the courage to get on with life physically, but emotionally I was still shrouded in sadness at it all. But each day, I somehow dragged myself out of bed and reminded myself of the saying *"There is only one courage, and that is the courage to go on dying to the past. Not to collect it, not to accumulate it, not to cling to it. We all cling to the past, and because we cling to it we become unavailable to the present"*. I would put on my brave mask and just keep on trying.

The road to the mountains from Aberdeen passes a gliding club, and I imagined soaring above the hills with the freedom of a bird. I wondered if it might help fill my void. I joined the

University gliding club, which meant an affordable experience was possible, and drove out to the airfield on a frozen winter weekend with Pete and Isla, feeling apprehensive but excited about my first engine-less flight. We sat around for hours, waiting for a glider slot, but eventually I pushed across the hard, frosted ground towards a cockpit. I sat in the front with the instructor behind and donned my goggles and scarf whilst the lid was pulled down over us. We were encapsulated and I felt a lurch of concern as we were tied on a line to a small plane, which began bouncing us across the grassy airfield. We raced across the ground and the glider's nose twitched disconcertingly up, then down, then finally up, up and away. The plane dropped us off tow and our giant white wings soared above the Cairngorms, their sugar-lump contours dotted with icy lochs, just tiny puddles from our sky-high view. The mountains looked distant and serene, but too far away to really feel a connection. I couldn't feel the spirit of the mountains. Only the rush of cold air and a niggling concern at the rattling sheets of fibreglass that somehow held us in the land of birds.

The glider had dual controls, just like a driving instructor's car. I took over control of steering and played at tweaking the glider's nose up and down, left to right, testing its sensitivity. Disappointed at my lack of connection with the wildness we flew over, I was a junkie craving adrenaline. The glider nose swung heavenward and my stomach jumped into my chest. The instructor took over the controls, and I asked if we could do some acrobatics. Suddenly, we were upside down, the world inverted and then we were pointing with wing to the ground, spiralling fast, the ground spinning and my head dizzy. I laughed so loudly that no sound came out. I was just a grinning, air-flattened face as my body was pinned back with the acceleration as the air furiously ripped around the glider.

Fifteen minutes after we'd launched, we were landing again. I'd had a major adrenaline fix. I felt happy with the blast of escapism, but it all seemed so short. As we descended sedately towards the airfield, the instructor informed me that he would try and land the glider without using his feet on the rudder, to test if it was possible for me to fly alone, with only my hands. His enthusiasm to help me get airborne was heartening, but as the grassy fields rushed towards us and we started wobbling, I realized that we weren't quite where we should be. I braced myself as the wheels missed the smooth grassy strip and hit the rough turf of the field. We sped towards the river, the glider jolting and bouncing, and I tensed and clutched the seat on either side of me. I waited, helpless and nervous, for a collision, but fortunately, we slowed to a stance without hitting anything. "It was a bit tricky landing the glider without a rudder", my instructor announced through the headset-intercom that connected us. As if I hadn't noticed!

It had been an exciting experience, but I decided gliding wasn't for me in the long-term. I didn't think I would enjoy all the waiting around for a fifteen minute slot in the air, and couldn't see myself spending hours polishing and maintaining a prized white bird. And I'd been disappointed at how drifting above the mountains felt so different and distant in comparison to being in them. I searched urgently for another activity.

Horse-riding seemed like it might be a good way of getting into the forests and hills. I imagined trekking through glens and emerging above the trees onto the open heather tops. I wheeled through a horse-dung covered yard, towards a young wax-jacketed, green-wellied woman leading a handsome horse towards me. I felt sure this would be the key to some freedom in the hills. Smiles and greetings over, she directed me to a concrete platform from which I would mount the steed that towered above me. From my chair, I tossed one leg over the horse's back and with some shoving and pulling of various limbs by the collection of stable-hands, I arrived in the saddle.

I was clueless. The wax-jacket lady led the horse, while I concentrated on balancing. My unusable abdominal muscles meant I was a wobbling weeble and I clung to the horse's neck as my bum slid sideways off the saddle, like a dying cowboy clinging to his horse. It was hard to maintain any posture and when we tried to trot, I felt like a sack of potatoes slumped on the horse whilst every bone and organ churned.

I tried riding on a few more occasions, but each time I dismounted with piercing upper backache and a sense that I'd survived the experience rather than enjoyed it, let alone developed any skill. On my final ride, I got so saddle-sore I feared my chaffed bottom would never mend and I spent most of the next week lying on my stomach in bed letting my damaged skin heal. I had no passion for taking up horse-riding on a serious or regular basis.

In all the activities I tried, I had to be vigilant about my skin. My lack of sensation meant that I couldn't tell if I'd scratched or scuffed myself and with poor circulation to my lower body I had to be very careful to avoid damage. Sitting on an injured backside could create huge pressure sores, killing the flesh through to the bone. I'd shared the hospital ward with patients who had sores the size of dinner plates on their bottoms, waiting for silicon implants, muscle transplants and skin grafts and who'd sometimes had to lie on their fronts for a year or more waiting for their holes to heal.

I felt marginalised from so many mainstream activities and struggled to overcome the barriers of equipment and training that the clubs or groups I wanted to join could not easily meet. I missed the ease of meeting like-minded people, and getting to know them in an outdoor 'in-it-together' environment. But I wasn't ready for the prospect of an inactive life and from somewhere, I found energy to keep inventing ways of staying active.

I'd always been a fan of cycling and enjoyed exploring places by bike. I liked the sensation of the wind in my hair as the landscape flashed by and the physical reward of pedalling somewhere. I'd even enjoyed the sweating and labouring of climbing a hill, straining my muscles when I couldn't get the bike into bottom gear. It was a sport I missed and which I thought had opportunities for solving my quest for freedom.

Unfortunately any piece of specialized mobility equipment costs close to a few thousand pounds and a hand-pedalled bike had a price tag that made me gulp. I thought about what I really wanted from a bike, and how much I had loved cycle touring. Maybe a hand bike, if it had chunky tyres, could go off-road and help me discover new places.

I suspected that an arm-powered bike could never go at the same pace as a regular bike and that if I cycle-toured with a friend they would get cold and frustrated at the slow pace. I settled on the idea of a tandem. If it could be designed so that my arms pedalled in synch with a partner's legs then each of us could adjust our effort according to our energy levels – they wouldn't get bored and cold, and I wouldn't get left behind!

I searched on the Internet for something that resembled my

idea. Greenspeed was an Australian company who made recumbent bikes and also sold a single hand-pedalled recumbent tricycle. I phoned them, and after a long chat to Ian, the founder and design enthusiast, I was ready to order a tandem recumbent tricycle with hand-pedals at the front, and foot-pedals at the back. It was an expensive piece of equipment, but I was lucky to be granted a significant amount of the cost by a trust that support sportsmen and women back into sport after an accident. I was excited about the creation that was now being built and didn't even consider the risks of not being able to test this expensive tool of freedom. I was focused purely on the outcome – the ability to cycle, to tour and to travel.

I was now almost two years back into my PhD and had gathered some interesting results. As fortune would have it, I was asked to speak at a geological conference in 'Surfer's Paradise' in Australia, and seized it as an opportunity to pick up the giant bike. When the work was over, I traveled to 'Ferntree Gully', a quaint sounding village on the outskirts of Melbourne. Here, in the garage of a regular-looking house, a very irregular bike was waiting for me. I was slightly nervous as Ian, the mad-keen bearded bike builder, lifted the garage door, to reveal my three metre long ticket to freedom. Would it fit me? Would I be able to pedal it? Would it get up the hills that I had in mind? More immediately, would I get it on the plane home?

He proudly wheeled it out; two bright yellow deck-chair-like seats invited me to ride. I climbed aboard and whizzed downhill. Careering around a bend a few minutes later, I knew the bike was what I had been looking for. I christened it 'The Green Beast' in honour of its frame colour and ungainly size and shape. On leaving Australia a few weeks later, I smiled sweetly at the airline check-in desk and was shocked when they checked in the Green Beast without more than a slightly raised eyebrow. I was even more surprised that it actually fitted through the door into the luggage hold of the plane.

My first real tour with the Green Beast was to the Outer Hebrides. I'd long wanted to visit this collection of islands off the west coast of Scotland, and my friend Lesley and I planned a four-day tour of the islands of Harris and Uist as a testing ground for greater things.

We frantically threw our gear into a pile at the ferry port as the boat honked its horn ready to leave. Lesley ran, pushing the tandem onto the boat and I chased after. Standing on the deck, we looked down at the Green Beast, parked alongside trucks and cars. It was ridiculously long for a bike and with the tent tied on its front, protruding like a figurehead, the grand machine looked even longer.

I was amazed that the huge pile of gear, when packed and tied neatly, fitted onto the back of the bike in two neat panniers. We strapped the sleeping mats on top and then the wheelchair, its seat filled with food and water. It was a precarious pile balanced on the back but after a few hundred metres of pedalling along the road we were happy that cycling it was possible. We slowly ate the miles of gently undulating coastal road around North Uist, enjoying the tail wind that whisked us the ten miles to the next ferry for Harris.

It felt fantastic being away from the confines of a car, appreciating the sun and wind on my face, and a view without the shield of glass. It was the injection of freedom I had been searching for. Self-contained and self-reliant, we clicked through

Cycling the "Green Beast", Outer Hebrides, August 1996

the lanes of Harris, dazzled by the white glare of its silver beaches and mesmerized by the deep turquoise of the shallow sea. The sea was mirror calm and its horizon blended into the sky, small distant islands hanging like clouds in the midst of the scape. It was magical.

As we negotiated the circumference of Harris, reaching its rocky eastern shore and series of tea and Harris Tweed shops, we met tourists tootling along the lanes in their cars. They were shocked to see this bizarre machine moving towards them, and we were barraged with questions that seemed progressively more stupid as we cranked along.

"My, what a super machine"

"Wow, look at that. What is it?"

"Does it go on the road?" (as we cycled along the road towards them.)

"How many people does it take?", (as Lesley and I sat on its two bright yellow seats.)

The Green Beast was an object of great public interest, and we soon became used to the "oohs" and "aahs" as we cycled through villages, avoiding as much as possible the waves of inquiry. With the wheelchair hidden in the pile on the back of the bike, no-one realized that I couldn't walk. Most people just thought we were slightly odd choosing to pedal such a strange contraption, and suggested that we swap positions so that we could get a full body workout! If I got into my chair under the eyes of intrigued observers, I would see their thoughts change from "Look at those posers on that bike" to "Oh, what a shame. How brave of you to cycle". I really didn't want their sympathy.

In the grassy sand dunes of the isle of Berneray we camped overlooking a white crescent of beach. The water, islands and distant hills of Skye were a blend of greys, their colours bleached and musty in the dusk. I lay in the tent with the soothing lullaby of surf washing onto the beach. I felt I'd found a perfect paradise in this land of water and peaceful islands.

The following day I had an unexpected opportunity to get closer to the sea with a kayaking-mad gang at the outdoor centre in North Uist. I was offered a place in a double sea kayak and joined a rainbow crowd of elegant crafts to paddle over the glassy water. We kayaked ten miles offshore to the seal-blanketed Monarch Islands, one of the last ports of call before the mighty expanse of Atlantic. I fell in love with the freedom of being able to go anywhere on the water, with the sounds of the sea and the shear scale of the marine wilderness. We surfed a wave and somehow didn't capsize and lunched on a white beach with rich turquoise water. The sun shone bright and I was in heaven.

It was peaceful. It was wild. It felt free.

So, I settled on the formula of cycling and kayaking, but I also found a winter addition – skiing. Scotland's Alternative Skiers are an organization that was key to seeing me through my first winters back in Scotland. Regular weekends away with a collection of strange and wonderful skiing equipment and a very diverse group of characters became a lifeline to me whilst my other friends were heading away to ice climb and walk in the mountains.

We would meet at one of the Scottish ski centres – Glenshee, Cairngorm or Aonach Mor, and if we were lucky, managed to ski. I was both excited and frustrated at my skills of mastering a mono ski-bob – essentially a seat mounted on a single ski with a shock absorber, and two short 'outrigger' skis for the arms. In the beginning it felt suicidal to launch myself down a slope without the ability to stop or turn, my level of control over the ski equivalent to a jelly wobbling on a knife. But slowly, with the patience of the volunteers and various friends who were willing to come and pluck me out of fences and ditches, I began to learn how to control the plank beneath me.

Getting back up the mountainside was more of an ordeal than skiing down. A collection of ropes and clips attached to the ski and looped around the T-bars. The jolt of the tow as it pulled into tension sent me rocketing skywards before a painful reunion with the hard snow. If I managed to survive 'take-off' the next challenge was to stay balanced whilst being dragged through the ruts. When I fell, I inevitably caused a pile-up of bodies and skis, hijacking happy skiers on the tow behind me. On the rare occasion that I reached the top of the tow without event, I could pull a quick release rope that would unclip the loop and leave me free to ski off down the slope. But the timing of release was critical – if I released too early then I found myself skiing backwards, too late and I

Learning to sit-ski, Glenshee, Scotland

would be wrestling with the mechanics of the ski tow.

On my first trip to the Alps, I watched with envy as other ski-bobs whizzed past me, in awe of the skills it took to gain that level of control. But with determined practice, I began to master the chairlifts and the skiing. Within a few years, I was there too, smiling with sheer joy at the sensation of flying down the mountain slopes, still hardly able to believe that I had finally mastered the contraption in which I sat. I felt very thankful to Scotland's Alternative Skiers for their existence and support. Now I was able to enjoy the winter mountains too.

Phheeww. I'm sure you're exhausted with hearing about all that, as I know I was, in trying to do it all. I think I somehow felt that I had to make up for the things I couldn't do anymore. I had to prove something. Shit, I was still playing out that pattern of striving to achieve that I'd become vaguely aware of years before. What I haven't told you is that during those years, I sustained injury after injury. I broke my leg, I broke my hip, I spent chunks of time lying on my front to avoid skin damage becoming a pressure sore, I had wires removed from the original broken elbow that all the activity had aggravated... I mean, retrospectively, I was pushing myself too hard, and just falling back into the same old pattern, piling on stress and pressure to achieve. I guess we all have patterns that mean we keep repeating the same mistakes. I realize now that I was 'stuck' in a way of being, a way of behaving that was driven by my head and a need to physically achieve, and it didn't seem to be doing me any good. But I didn't get any of that then!

With the combination of cycling, sea kayaking and skiing, I was happy that I could leave the frantic pace of the man-made world whenever I wanted and touch the freedom and peace that I yearned for. From the expanse of the sea, I could somehow feel how large the world is, how wide its horizons. Being able to experience this again allowed me to temper the emotional highs and lows of life, and gently seek perspective. The vastness of the wilderness allowed me to see everything else as small. My sadness lost its importance. Whatever I'd lost remained out there somewhere, and I felt part of something great. The wilderness gave me humility, inspiration and energy to embrace my new life.

Handcycling in the 70 Wild Miles race, Glen Etive, Scotland

CHAPTER 7

'WHAT IF ?'

"You don't get to choose how you're going to die. Or when. You can only decide how you're going to live. Now."

JOAN BAEZ

The morning sun cast a bright glow through the yellow nylon fabric, its weak heat intensified within the confines of the tent. The brightness beckoned my eyelids to open and seconds later I unzipped my Arctic-rated sleeping bag to expel the heat from its feathers and lay there in semi-consciousness. The heat soon ousted me from my land of snooze. I slid, on my bottom, through the flaps and zips of tent, into the sunshine.

I dragged my sleeping mat from the tent, positioned it towards the sun and collapsed onto it again, closing my eyelids to blissful rays. A light breeze kept the deathly nips of the Scottish midges at bay. The previous night I'd come under their vampire attack and now scratched the raging bites they'd left on my arms and neck. I was strangely glad that my lack of sensation concealed the relentless itch that must have plagued the collection of red lumps around my ankles.

My eyes accustomed to the brightness and I lazily surveyed

our camp spot. Sandy cliffs cast their long morning shadow beside me, small grassy ledges breaking their precipice. A few strides away, the sea broke onto a golden beach. A grassy peninsula bound the beach at one end, with a rocky rise at its furthest point. Nestled between the sea and the cliffs, our hamlet of tents, with its unzipped doors and protruding limbs, showed vague signs of life. There were seven tents and, I counted in my mind, fifteen of us on this midsummer camping pilgrimage to the Northern Scottish coast.

We'd arrived late the previous night and put our tents up in the dark. They now looked crooked and haphazard. Some of us planned to paddle in sea kayaks and others to climb the cliffs.

My eyes strayed back to the short peninsula ahead of me. I studied its rocky bump, contemplating the possibility of 'bumming' to its insignificant summit. I laughed inside. No-one else would even notice there was a rise, but I was considering a route up through its rocky slopes as if it was some unscaled Himalayan mountain. My new perspective meant I noticed things that others missed – challenge was all relative.

A paraplegic guy I'd met recently had just bummed up Ben Nevis. It took him four days to reach the summit and dozens of pairs of gloves, which had been ripped apart by the sharp rocky paths. I was utterly impressed with his feat and since I'd heard about it, had dreamt of reaching a mountain summit again under my own steam. Four days seemed like a gruelling epic compared to the usual four hours it took on legs, but I was still tempted. Perhaps this small rise could be my initiation in uphill bumming. I thought of a small hill behind Aberdeen beach and targeted it as my stage two training ground. Maybe I'd be bumming up a real

Scottish mountain by the end of the summer.

From my distant viewing point, I scrutinized the short slope. There was a diagonal line across a rocky slab. If I followed it, it would lead me to some hummocky ground that looked negotiable. Planning my route of attack, I recalled climbing guidebooks that described routes by each intricate move. Insignificant slopes now replaced the vertical or overhanging rock faces of the classic climbing guide. Regardless of size or steepness, it seemed equally challenging. In fact, now, everywhere I looked were challenges.

Bodies began to emerge from the tents. Stoves bubbled morning cups of tea and calorie-loaded plastic bags littered the camp and rustled in the breeze. Three balanced meals a day always merged into a continuous eating extravaganza during camping trips, good nutrition punctuated by excessive junk, inevitably involving chocolate.

Pete and Isla were camped beside me. We contemplated the day over a prolonged breakfast. Most of the group wanted to climb on the sea cliffs, the colourful gathering of tents already strewn with ropes and climbing necessities. The symbolic chink of the metal gear resounded against the quiet morning. I'd almost forgotten the once familiar sound; a trigger for cutting memories that I needed to leave behind.

Pete hadn't climbed since our last dramatic day at the sea cliffs. We turned to examine the sea together. It looked calm with only a gentle rolling swell and no sign of white caps. It was a perfect day for exploring the nooks and caves of the coastline in the kayaks.

Unable to assist with carrying the kayaks down to the beach,

I decided to embark on my 'Himalayan' route. The peninsula was closer to the beach and it would be easier to hitch a piggy-back from there, across the sand to the boats. I pulled on some waterproof trousers. I thought their slippery fabric would help me slide my backside across the grass.

The first few moves were mere shuffles, the weight of my legs and drag of my heels a severe hindrance to progress. I discovered that if I bent my knees and pushed up on my hands, then my bum was projected backwards as my legs straightened. I refined my technique with each move, and across the flat ground I made quite fast progress, relative to the snails I passed in the sandy grass.

As the gradient increased, the technique meant that my bum was launched into the slope and I lost my balance and wobbled forwards onto my knees. I switched to short shuffles, and then wished I wasn't wearing such smooth fabric, as I seemed to slide back down the grass almost as far as each move took me. I tried some sideways shuffles with my legs following the contour of the hill, but then I just lost my balance and ended up rolling back down the slope.

It was a molehill of a challenge, but my frustration welled, along with amazement at how anyone had managed to bum to the top of Britain's highest mountain! I dreamt of having abdominal muscles that worked, convinced that it would make this whole uphill bumming malarkey more feasible. But there was no way that I was letting such a pathetic lump beat me. I persevered.

After much blundering and swearing at my legs, feeling angry at the useless weight they added to the task, I somehow made it to the top. My drive to get there was rooted in frustration and anger. My whole hour of endeavour had taken a very circuitous route to avoid steep slopes and rocks. From the outstanding altitude I'd achieved, the view was little different from that at the base. It wasn't quite the panorama that would have rewarded an hour of walking uphill.

I looked down at the beach where the kayaks queued patiently for activity. I lay back in the grass, exhausted and disillusioned with the viability of a full mountain-bumming expedition.

Pete and Adam joined me and the three of us sat, looking back to the cliffs where the others had finally begun climbing. We aimlessly chatted, switching our attention from the cliffs to the sea, lethargically avoiding getting into the kayaks. We watched Scott climbing on the cliff nearest to us. He was too distant to see clearly – just a purple form with four outstretched limbs against the sunlit rock, picking his route slowly up the face.

A puffin distracted me, flapping its wings energetically as it skimmed the water. I laughed at its humorous style, and in that moment, realized that I was beginning to appreciate the pleasure in simple things again. Maybe my paralysis wouldn't consume me forever.

Looking back to the cliffs, Scott was just one move from the grass that highlighted the cliff top. I watched him, mulling my thoughts to the lull of the sea, swashing and stirring pebbles. He moved his right arm quickly upwards, his speed hinting at anxiety and urgency to reach the solid safety of the grass. His hand grappled for a sturdy hold but he couldn't find anything solid.

I could almost feel the gritty ball bearings beneath my fingertips, safety sliding fast from my grasp. The cliff top rolled away, fingers clawing for help.

I watched him falling out into a void. I saw each metal attachment rip smoothly from the rock.

In those few seconds as a helpless spectator, a bullet round of images ricocheted through my mind. Images of walking, running, climbing, falling, lying, bleeding. I sat immersed in helplessness as the event unfolded before me. Powerless to act, help or control the situation in any way.

The chunk of time missing from my memory played before me. It was like watching a film of my own accident. Even the setting was similar – a Sunday morning at the sea cliffs. The place where he landed was hidden from my view but I had an image of his body, battling and bleeding, paralysed. Silent trickles leaked from the corners of my eyes as I sat alone on my insignificant rise. Pete and Adam had long since sprinted to the cliff. I could just see their heads behind some boulders that obscured my view.

I felt once again the fragility of the tightrope we all walk. One slip, one small moment, and everything changes. Dead or paralysed?

A yellow wasp buzzed into sight, the same type of chopper that had rescued me. It hovered between me and the cliff, giant and deafening, exactly like the one that had rescued me. My hair blew wildly in the draft of the blades, grass flattened and camping debris scattered. The calm peace of the Sunday morning was drenched by its presence, a symbol of both disaster and hope.

Paramedics jumped from the chopper. There was commotion and concern everywhere. They joined the others behind the boulders and all I could see was a crowd of heads. Distant from it, the scene was a blur as more and more people gathered. I glimpsed a flash of purple.

It was Scott. His head was amongst the others. He was alive! He was standing! A hurricane of relief swept through my body. Then surprise. The cliff was higher than the one I'd fallen from. How come he was okay? I focused again on the crowd, and was relieved to see that Scott was definitely at the heart of it. Everyone moved into full view, heading away from the cliffs towards the camp. I eventually got back into my wheels and with help, rejoined the others. Scott hobbled over to me as his foot was badly bashed, and laid on some camping mats. He looked at me and said, very simply, "Sorry". At that moment the bright yellow chopper arrived. Scott shook his head and despite some persistence on the part of the 'emergency' crew, he didn't want to be flown away in the rescue-bird.

Sorry? Why did he feel sorry, I wondered? Sorry that I had been paralysed in a similar incident? Sorry that I'd seen everything? It had certainly been strange, watching the scene, almost like a replay of my own accident, but I only noticed relief in myself that Scott was okay.

One slip, one small moment, and he was neither dead nor paralysed. His tightrope must have been made of stronger fibres than mine.

Destiny? Fate? Luck? Who controls this play that is our lives?

I was happy for him. I was sad for myself. I was sadder for Will.

The scene played in my mind, over and over again.

The following weekend, on another of my now frequent camping trips to the west coast of Scotland, I stared into the glowing embers of a campfire, its waning flames dancing gently. My face was close and my eyes stung with the heat and my intense gazing at the blue heart of the fire. The bright aura of a Scottish summer night persisted and the sound of the sea rhythmically washing the beach hypnotized me. I was oblivious to the conversation around me, the voices drowned by those that chattered in my mind. Absorbed by the flickering colours of the fire, I reflected.

Last Sunday, when Scott fell, had been an odd day. After the fall, he had gone by car to the local hospital. They hadn't found anything wrong, but a few days later, with some pain, he'd gone to Aberdeen hospital for an X-ray. He had a stable fracture of the spine, but luckily not damaged his spinal cord.

It seemed like a very weird sequence of events. Three random Sundays, and three random falls, all within a year of each other. First me, with a small but devastating break of my spine. Yet something had kept my heart pumping blood to my otherwise massacred body. Then Will; one loose rock and he had plummeted to his death. Now Scott, with another small, but less devastating crack in his spine, and he could walk away.

What if I hadn't gone climbing that day? What if we'd gone North instead of South? What if we'd chosen a different route? What if Will hadn't gone climbing again? What if, what if, what if?

I was filled with endless 'What ifs?'. Split second decisions and actions had led each of us to an entirely different destiny. Why? My thoughts hovered around in circles, and it was an infinite, fruitless trail to pursue the question of 'What if?'. Maybe I was really thinking "If only!"

"We all walk a different path in life, led by our dreams and actions." The fire crackled. "Do we have complete control of our own reality? Are there moments when the outcome is somehow predetermined?" That's how it was starting to feel – that we weren't the only force in the driving seat of our own destiny. I had a feeling that somewhere, somehow, a greater plan was at work.

The question that took hold in my mind next was not "What if?" but "So what?" What to make of all this?

The glow of the embers faded, along with my thoughts, chased by the cold of a starry Scottish night.

"So what?"

CHAPTER 8

HOW? NOW. WOW!

"What we vividly imagine, ardently desire, enthusiastically act upon, must inevitably come to pass."
COLIN P. SISSON

I'd been back in Aberdeen for three years now and my geology PhD was coming to an end. Apart from wondering what I would do next and how I would earn some money, and that question of 'so what?' that had seated itself inside me with respect to the 'meaning of life', there was one burning desire that I couldn't ignore. I was desperate to visit the 'big' mountains, but not just to see them. I wanted to be part of them in some way. I could go off-road on the Green Beast and enjoy escape from the concrete-world for a while. If its robust frame could negotiate Cairngorm mountain tracks, then I saw no reason why it couldn't tackle something larger.

So there I was, spending a series of winter nights nestled in front of a fire with a stack of travel books, scheming some crazy idea to cycle through Central Asia and the Himalaya. Despite others' scepticism, and my own doubt, the idea wouldn't dissolve. Part of me had already learned that if we set ourselves a goal, no matter how 'impossible' it may seem, with time, patience, focus and determination we can achieve things we previously wouldn't have believed. So, although there was that voice inside saying "What do you think you're doing? How are you ever going to do that?" there was another voice there, quieter to begin with, yet persistently determined, saying "That would be amazing, and if you plan and prepare for it well, you'll do it."

This battle of voices within me went on. The 'negative' voice tried to persuade me how dangerous it was, how unrealistic I was being, how ridiculous it was to think that I could manage something like this, how irresponsible I was being. It filled me with fear and almost stopped me from going ahead with the planning. Yet the 'positive' voice within me grew louder the more I listened to it. It told me how with careful planning, lots of training so that I was physically fit, using the right equipment and being mentally prepared, we would have an amazing time.

Probably it's normal to experience that duo of voices, one telling us to stop, that we'll never manage it, and the other, attracted to the goal or the outcome, driving us forward telling us how great it will be to reach this 'future picture'. And we always have a choice about which voice to listen to. It's just a simple matter of recognising that we have a choice, then deciding where to put our energy. We can spend our time and energy focusing on the fear and the 'what if's', or focus on the possibility and the belief that we can actually achieve that thing we secretly dream of.

I noticed that on days that I listened to the negative voice, I felt flat, down, fed-up and de-motivated. And on the days that I took heed of the other voice, and just got on with planning as if it were happening, I felt buoyant, energised, purposeful and motivated. I was struck by how much my mind could control my mood, and hence my whole experience of the world in a day. When

I chose the "you can do it" attitude, I felt better, seemed to have more energy, and took action. And when I focused on the "can't do it" voice I felt more sluggish, more tired, and achieved less in a day.

Maybe I just wanted the goal so badly that I managed to ignore the negative voice, and something within me kept imagining what it would feel like to be in the giant mountains, speeding downhill, wind in my hair, with all the majesty and beauty of the glaciers and snow-capped peaks like an amphitheatre above and all around. My imagination drove me forward and the power of the voice in my head kept me going, and planning, even when the doubtful part of me started chattering away.

After months of hard work, planning, saving and learning about bicycle maintenance, Lesley, Pete, Gheorghe and I found ourselves on a plane destined for Kazakhstan – four cyclists with the aim of crossing the Karakoram mountains at the western end of the Himalaya. With the Green Beast, two mountain bikes and a trailer for the chair, we felt apprehensive and wondered if we should have been more sceptical than we had about the task ahead. We planned to cycle from Kyrgyzstan over the Tien Shan mountains into China, then along the Karakoram Highway via the towering height of the Khunjerab Pass, the gateway into Pakistan. We would be roughing it all the way, just wild-camping and eating very basic camp food. People often ask me how I afford all these trips, but its only through spending carefully at home, saving and living in such a basic way whilst abroad, that they are possible. After the cost of the flight it is often cheaper to be away than at home because the cost of living drops so dramatically when life is reduced to the simplicity of a tent and self-powered transport.

A Kazakh official picked me up from my seat and carried me, unflinchingly, from the plane, holding me on the landing strip for another fifteen minutes whilst the airline crew searched for my wheelchair. I never thought I could feel relieved at the sight of it, but it did provide me with movement, and I'd eventually become attached to it. It had now moulded to fit me just like a comfortable pair of shoes.

At immigration stern-faced, suited-officials informed us, "Sorry, but you will have to take the next plane back to your country. Your visas are not valid."

"What!" Lesley exclaimed, as she'd worked so hard arranging logistics for our trip.

We checked our passports, and sure enough, the visas were not valid for another week. We begged and pleaded, but they weren't budging. Finally we pulled out some dollars and everything changed. We were in!

We squeezed our bikes and bodies into a mini-van bound for Bishkek, the capital of Kyrgyzstan, and bounced our dusty way toward the city. It felt a great adventure as we gathered food and equipment for the few months that lay ahead. I remembered the time, lying in a hospital bed, when I had thought that adventure like this would never be possible again – and certainly not a journey into some of the world's highest mountains.

Our first few days of cycling didn't bode well for a successful journey. Every few kilometres a bolt or a piece of metal, vital to the smooth running of our bikes, clinked onto the rough tarmac. A critical nut that kept my hand-pedal attached went missing, and all the jolting and jarring over the rough road surface caused the bottle rack to shear off the frame. Doubts crept into me. Were we being realistic about undertaking this journey, with a thousand miles of dirt road ahead? Maybe I should have listened to that negative voice after all.

But we weren't turning back and to keep our cycling dream alive we improvised in every possible way. We used chewing gum to temporarily stop the hand-pedal from falling off and we got into a habit of tightening all the vital nuts and bolts on our bikes each evening.

My arm muscles ached as we cranked through the miles. I recalled the first time I'd ever tried to hand-cycle around a park in Aberdeen. Even after a few hundred metres I'd felt exhausted and wondered how my arms could ever power me any distance. I hadn't known at the time how easily the body adapts if you are persistent with training and that I would one day find myself able to hand-pedal thousands of miles. I though it would be funny to be named like the great cyclist Lance *Armstrong*.

We'd managed to find an old military map of Kyrgyzstan in

Cycling through the Tien Shan Mountains, Kyrgyzstan, August 1997

Britain, but it bore little resemblance to the one that we'd bought in Bishkek. We didn't know which one to believe, and the only common road between them lead east towards a giant Lake called Issy-Kul, where we would turn south into the rising Tien Shan mountains. It wasn't the motorway that we'd expected, and there was more horse traffic than trucks negotiating its appalling surface. The heat was intense and our wheels left tyre tracks in the semi-molten tar.

Farmers and travellers smiled at us, and children playing in the villages we passed through screamed hilariously at the sight of our bicycle caravan. At the end of our first long sweaty day, we found a good place to camp in a grassy orchard beside the road. We settled into the idyllic shady spot as dusk descended, and only the occasional rumble of a passing truck tainted the deep sleep that our bodies sank into.

At dawn, we woke to a collection of very flat tyres, riddled with multi-pronged thorns that had been hidden in the grass. We fixed all the punctures but didn't realize that thorns were embedded deep in the rubber of the tyres – we spent the next two days intermittently mending holes. We avoided camping in thorn fields from then on!

Our Lonely Planet guidebook informed us that when the USSR collapsed and the Kyrgyz gained independence in 1991, the country opened to foreigners and the people were learning fast about tourism. The country was apparently ninety percent mountainous – we must have been following the only flat road it had, and the kind, curious approach of the locals suggested that not too many tourists had been there.

The Kyrgyz people were incredibly welcoming and friendly,

always willing to share the little they had and insistent that we stayed in their family homes. Our Russian was appalling, but still a vast improvement on our Kyrgyz, and communication involved a lot of amateur dramatics with exaggerated hand symbols and facial expressions. They looked amazed when the skeleton of metal carried in the trailer behind Lesley's bike gained wheels and I clambered out of the bike into it. Most evenings, we were ushered into a family's simple home, given nan bread and kumus – the national drink of sour horse milk which we drank under disguised protest – and then offered a colourful, deep layer of mattresses and elaborate blankets on which to rest our weary muscles.

The hours we spent cycling each day gave me a new sense of freedom, as we cruised through fields and rolling hills towards an inspiring horizon of snow-capped mountains. In the hours that we spent 'in the saddle' I felt myself shedding sadness and coming alive with the beauty of my surroundings. In the last few years I'd sometimes felt imprisoned in my own body - sitting in the same chair, in the same position. Trivial though it may seem, the bike with the rotation of my arms, the stretch of my legs, and the wind through my hair all made me feel just a tiny bit more free.

The Dolon Pass was our first gruelling encounter with the mountains. The road surface deteriorated, lacking asphalt and gaining a depth of gravel. Lesley struggled to balance the trailer over the rough ground and the Green Beast was heavy and slow with wheel spin. We resorted to pushing, and I worried again about the road ahead. Would we make it all the way to Pakistan?

The town of Naryn nestled in dry sandy hills that resembled a Hollywood Western stage set. It was our last chance to replenish supplies before the remote stretch into the At Bashi and Tien Shan mountains. We stayed in an old sewing machine factory, now converted into a hostel, which had beds for a few dollars, and we met our first tourists, who also happened to be cyclists.

They had just returned from the Torugart Pass, which was our route into China. They had cycled all the way there, and then been refused entry and sent back to Naryn. We knew that crossing the border was a challenge in itself, and our research had told us that we'd need both a fax from China 'inviting' us into the country and for a Chinese organisation to meet us at the pass. We had spent hours at home, planning things, faxing back and forth to arrange for a Chinese tourist organisation to meet us at the border. We'd had to specify a certain date and time for the meeting, and felt pressured by our need to arrive at the border for that day, especially with all the uncertainty of the road surface and our speed.

As we heard the others' stories of woe – not only having been sent back, but also fined by the Office of Visas and Immigration for not having the correct registration stamp in their passports, we were glad of all our preparation. We just hoped that the collection of stamps, visas and papers that we carried would be enough to appease the border officials at Torugart.

Not far from Naryn, the string of villages ended, the tarmac ran out, and we entered a remote, tough land. The road led, dry, windswept and barren, into the mountains. The sun was hot and the landscape gave us nowhere to shelter. In the freezing nights I buried deep into my down clothes and sleeping bag. There were no streams for water, and we relied on the generosity of the local herdsmen who knew where to find springs, miles into the mountains from the road. Our diet was dull and simple – just nan bread pasted in cream and sugar with scrapings of our remaining Marmite, kumus to drink, and porridge and dried soup we'd brought from home to supplement the basic local fare.

I didn't notice any hardship. Each day it felt so incredible, just being in such a wild place. The miles of emptiness, feeling exposed to the elements, managing to live and survive in such basic harsh conditions and the importance of realizing that I could cope medically without absolute sterility and perfection was a huge relief to me. The needs of paralysis, which I had thought tied me tightly to the man-made world, were loosening as if handcuffs had been unlocked.

The practicalities of going to the toilet had worried me more than anything prior to the trip and I had racked my brain for ideas on how to manage. My simple solution was an inflatable toilet seat and a plastic trowel. Each morning I would dig a small pit in the shelter of an empty tent shell, place my ring of air over it, and plonk myself on top. It wasn't ideal, but it worked, and I could perform my ablutions, fill the hole back up with soil and leave little trace of any disturbance.

Long days of pedalling took us to the outer Kyrgyz checkpoint where a few very cold and bored looking soldiers marked our arrival, sixty kilometres from 'no-man's land'. After all the stories, we expected an interrogation, but the soldiers just casually flicked through our passports and asked us to pose for a photograph with them. A few hundred metres along, an armed soldier shouted to us from the top of his lookout tower, and from his gestures we guessed he wanted to confiscate our films. He marched down to us, correct and official, but then broke into a broad smile and handed us a small camera. "Please, I want picture."

We were invited for tea by a group of road-workers, and then to stay with one of their families. We'd only cycled a short distance all day, the road surface rougher than ever, but it was biting cold with small dust storms swirling around us. We accepted the invitation and were taken on horseback for afternoon tea in a traditional Yurta – a circular tent used by the nomads that roam the high plains and mountains with horses and yaks.

We had an evening of nonsensical conversation with a constant stream of intrigued, vodka-swilling nomads clad in layers of skin and fur, entering and leaving the tent as if we were a sideshow provided for the local community. That night, lying in the Yurta with the wind flapping its skins and listening to the sounds of the vast nothingness outside, I felt at peace.

In a slow, bumpy crawl we progressed toward the border. A serene beautiful landscape unfolded, the mountains becoming gentler and almost distant. The scenery became even more remote and wild. The road was like a dusty washboard and the vibrations shook the cocktail of our bodies and bikes. A double electric fence with deserted watchtowers marked the border between China and the 'old' Russia, security slackened now that it was no longer impenetrable. The road stretched straight, long and flat through the wasteland.

We were saved the last inhospitable twenty kilometres by Lesley's bike. Her crank broke and our only get-out in the dusty isolation was to hitch a ride with a rare truck whose dust cloud we could see approaching. We clambered into a spine-chilling, high speed rallying truck with two drunk drivers. The wheelchair and bikes bounced in the back and we all clung on and prayed as we hurtled along the dirt road. I improvised to try and recover some safety in our situation, feigning sickness and threatening to vomit in the cab of the truck if they didn't slow down. The driver and his mate carried on glugging a clear deadly liquid, but they slowed down and we trundled, unscathed, into a litter of caravans and makeshift buildings – the camp in the high desert that marked the Torugart Pass.

The infamous border. We were two days early for our arranged crossing, so we took some welcome rest. It was no holiday camp. Shambled railway carriages were home to border officials and their families, and a bitter wind swirled dust storms between the caravans. Occasionally a local could be seen, huddled in a warm animal skin overcoat and dashing from a caravan to a ramshackle portacabin. The largest portacabins were the official buildings, housing workers, the rare tourist, and a canteen. Our food was finished, so we were forced to eat in the visitors 'restaurant', and sample their collection of bacteria, which gave us eggy burps and put us to bed with sickness.

The toilet was a wooden hut with a plank balanced precariously over a long trench. As the trench filled, the hut and plank were moved along. Fresh, airy and very spacious but, the others told me, not a good place to visit in darkness with a burning bottom. I dreaded the combination of lack of sensation and bowel control, with rotting intestines, a wheelchair and no toilet or washing facilities that I could use. Luckily, I stayed well in that department!

The 'no-man's land' between Kyrgyzstan and China was misty and wet as we cycled in sodden dirty waterproofs towards the official Chinese entry point. Lesley was still pushing her bike. "Would the agency be there to meet and greet us into China? Please don't let us be turned back all that way" I wished.

We entered China through a giant stone archway and the landscape, if it was possible given the rain, became more arid. It was a short descent from the archway to the Chinese officials, who formed a smart but curt contrast to the more casual, friendlier Kazakhs. They were disconcerted by the fact the Gheorghe's passport was Romanian whilst the fax had informed them to expect four British people. They demanded to inspect every item and corner of our baggage, rummaging thoroughly in our carefully jigsaw-packed panniers. Their officious style vexed us, but we had to subdue our tempers, smile courteously and hope that they would allow us into China.

It didn't look hopeful. There was no sign of the pre-arranged vehicle from the Chinese Tourist Agency and there was no way we were getting in without it. Surely it couldn't all end here, at this dreary, drizzly border post. I imagined retracing the previous weeks of desolate gravel roads, never to discover the mountain jewels on the highway to Pakistan.

We waited nervously under the scrutinising eyes of the green and red uniformed officials; some of whom we thought couldn't be older than sixteen. Maybe it was prettier here when the sun shone, but any signs of beauty were completely shrouded in cloud. A white mini-van pulled onto the concrete forecourt. It was for us!

Elated, we wedged everything into the tiny van, collapsed our bikes and baggage to the minimum size possible and leashed the Green Beast precariously on top. Despite the downhill route, we were glad not to be cycling again on the long stretch of dirt washboard desert road that descended into China. We had been rattled and shaken enough already, and the bumping van was a welcome relief. I wrapped a scarf around my nose to filter out the dust that filled the air, and settled in for the ride.

The road led to the main Chinese customs point, one hundred kilometres after the stone archway that marked the border. It was hard to take the Chinese officials seriously as we'd just seen them stumble out of pink bed-sheets and dress in vests and translucent silk shirts ready for official duties. It was impossible to suppress a grin whilst they solemnly inspected our passports and interrogated us. Much to our relief, we were not allowed to cycle the final section of corrugated road to the city of Kashgar, and were escorted there by the agency where they were officially allowed to 'release' us.

The colour and bustle of Kashgar was a stark contrast to the quiet repression of Kyrgyzstan. Bright displays of vegetables, bagels and unfamiliar foods tantalized our tastebuds after the monotony of nan bread and kumus we had consumed. The city was busy with travellers and tourists, and I no longer felt we were on an intrepid exploratory journey. Fixing Lesley's bike was easy given the number of bike shops lining the streets, and after enjoying the luxuries of civilisation for a few days, resting and filling our stomachs, we were ready for the next part of our journey.

The Karakoram Highway is 1300 kilometres of single-track, largely dirt road which threads its way through a knot of four great mountain ranges – the Pamir, Karakoram, Hindu Kush and Himalaya. I read that it had opened in the early 1980s after a trade agreement between China and Pakistan. The crumbling mountains had claimed thousands of lives during its construction and subsequently in the continuous efforts to keep the road open, clearing landslides and rock fall.

From Kashgar, the 'highway' crossed a dry, scorched section of the Taklamakan Desert, where amazingly we occasionally found taps to douse ourselves with cool water. From the plains, we began winding and climbing slowly upwards toward the giant sand-dune mountains of the Pamir. Herds of sheep frequently blocked our way as we ground our cranks through the Ghez canyon, higher and further into the mountains. The only campsites we could find were roadside gravel and sand pits. The roar of the churning brown water carving through the canyon and the scale of the peaks that emerged above it were mouth-gapingly impressive.

The people we met were mainly Uyghur – Kyrgyz or Tajik in descent, and their mud homes were adorned with colourful hand-woven rugs and wall hangings. The highway must have brought major changes to their way of life, and we didn't find them as friendly as the people we'd met in Kyrgyzstan. They preferred to try and sell us a wall hanging rather than invite us in for tea.

The cycling was tough – steep, slow and very hard work. We became constantly hungry and dreamt of food we knew we wouldn't see for a long time yet. Our staple diet changed from nan bread and kumus to doughballs and boiled eggs.

Weeks of cycling into thinning air and headwinds were beginning to take their toll as we plodded slowly onward and upward. We envied the occasional cyclists we met travelling in the opposite direction, carrying comparatively no kit, just cruising downhill for hundreds of kilometres. We met two German cyclists who had just come from the Khunjerab Pass, the high point and gateway to Pakistan.

"But it's very hard and high. Are you not catching a bus?" We felt insulted that, despite the fact they had just cycled over the pass, they deemed it too difficult for us with the Green Beast, trailer and wheelchair. Indignant, we were more determined than ever to reach the top.

On our final day of climbing, only twenty kilometres were left before what promised to be an exciting descent into Pakistan. The dry mountains had been coated with ice and camels grazed beside the glacier snouts as reminders that we were in a high desert. We had run out of doughballs and eggs the previous evening, and with nothing else to eat our stomachs rumbled in symphony. A nasty grinding noise came from Lesley's bike crank and it seized up just five kilometres from the summit. It didn't matter – she could walk and push at a pace quicker than the Green Beast could crawl.

We paused for passport inspection, a simple process compared with the trials of the Kyrgyz-China border. Young boys manned the border post – a paint-flaked caravan marked *Frontier Defence of China*, which had little hope of defending itself from a storm never mind an invasion! The young border guards must have heard our stomachs or noticed our tiredness and offered us plates of rice. We ate enthusiastically.

My arm muscles burned and I hung my head down with focus and effort. My hands were numb as the piercing cold penetrated my gloves, and my breath became short and sharp with the lack of oxygen to feed my muscles. It was a strenuous last stretch to the summit, with false tops and hidden bends moving our target further away, but sure enough, the glacier-draped peaks slowly diminished in size.

The gradient slackened and finally, we were at the summit plaque. We were silent with awe and achievement. I absorbed the majesty of the mountain panorama and wished that my friend Will

Descending the Hunza Valley, Karakoram, August 1997

was there to share it with us.

We didn't hang around at the top. The elation at having made it to the highest point was quenched by the vicious cold, and the hairpin descent that plunged into the Indus gorge looked far too exciting to put on hold.

Our tyres barely clung to the rubble-strewn switchbacks. Commanding summits loomed high and infinite lengths of scree threatened our route ahead. It surely had to rank as the most spectacular road in the world.

I closed my eyes and felt the air tickling my hair against my skin. I smelt the crisp purity of the altitude. Adrenaline flooded my body and I felt higher than the mountains. The further we descended, the more the peaks recovered their superiority and unbelievable size.

I had dreamt of this feeling. I had grieved for this feeling;

never thought I could touch it again. The intensity at which I felt alive was greater than ever. I wasn't climbing a rock face and what I was doing physically had changed, but the experience was just as bright; the texture just the same.

I realised that paralysis hadn't excluded me from the wilderness. The only threat to my freedom had been in my mind. I was in a fantastic dream, but this time it was real. I was overcome with joy.

Our first night in Pakistan was courtesy of the Khunjerab Security Force. It was a very grand title for a very laid back job – policing the peaceful, barely-inhabited upper part of the gorge (though it didn't stay that way for long – war broke out there the following year). The security guards held a quaint English tea party for us, with a surprise treat of chips! It was delicious but an overload for our shrunken stomachs.

Another temporary botch-job with glue and a hammer fixed Lesley's bike again, and we devoured kilometres in downhill cruising. The deeper we plunged into the Indus gorge, the higher the Karakoram towered. In the base of the gorge, a raging brown torrent carved through neat green terraces of fruit and potatoes, then vertical rock walls and scree stretched to mighty white summits five thousand metres above the valley bottom. The Hunza valley was a fertile and friendly change from the Chinese desert and altitude, and without the pressure of reaching border deadlines and high passes, we relaxed and indulged in the spectacular, almost surreal scenery.

The population increased the further down the gorge we journeyed. In the villages we were followed by crowds of school-children who chased after us, grabbing hold of anything they could reach, and shouting constantly "One pen". All day "One pen" echoed in our heads, until finally we were shouting it at each other. Despite the annoyance, we wished we had a bundle of pens to hand out to them, but all we had to offer was smiles and the occasional ride on the tandem.

Our staple diet changed again to dhal and chapattis. The appearance of food like porridge, cornflakes and omelettes, along with a few powerful curries, played havoc with our guts, forcing us to take some rest days. We stayed in small guesthouses more often than we camped, and the toilets were usually 'squat and hover' in design. I struggled with thoughts of how to adapt my inflatable toilet seat, and in a practice attempt I pumped the seat hard with air to keep me as high as possible above the grimy smelly ceramic floor. Unfortunately, mid-poo, the ring exploded, dropping me into the pungent pot. After that, I had to make-do with a wheelbarrow inner tube bought from a local store, its leaky valve forcing me to pump air into it constantly whilst undertaking ablutions, to save it from going flat. The personal care and hygiene problems were more challenging than the cycling.

It felt like we were on holiday after the hundreds of gruelling kilometres we'd come. We crossed two spectacular suspension bridges into Gilgit, the town we'd chosen as the end of our cycling adventure. We pitched our tents in a town centre travellers haunt, filled with aimless souls who'd been travelling for years and didn't know where home was any more. After long nights of sleeping in remote areas, it was a novelty to socialise, visit curry houses, and explore the streets with their trinket-filled shops. The tuneful wail of the town's mosques carried through the night air, an extreme contrast to the howling winds of the high mountains.

It was hard to stop. Cycling had become our way of life for the last two months and I really didn't want it to end. The mountains that had haunted me for so long had become real again and I felt happiness radiating within me at the knowledge that they were part of my life once more.

But there was one small niggle, like a pebble in my shoe, that I was reminded of when I looked at the thin stony paths that threaded their way from the valley towards the summits. I wished that I didn't have to feel the air of longing that they triggered in me. A part of me still wanted to be able to follow them and get to places that others could. The paths and summits reminded me of a deep frustration that I was trying hard to hide and forget; so deep that I almost missed noticing it. I certainly didn't know what to do with it, except ignore it.

Being in the big mountains was a defining journey for me and a huge personal achievement. I was elated to have visited such an awe-inspiring place, and to have been able to experience the rawness of its elements and to breathe its wildness. I had been playing hide and seek with myself, with my confidence, self-belief and self-esteem during the years since my accident. Our journey, as an independent unit of friends, travelling, surviving and exploring such a place, helped me to find myself again. Maybe I didn't need to be in such an exotic faraway place to do that, but it was definitely important to have a stretching goal to aim for. It was a goal that teetered on the brink of possibility, a dot on a distant horizon, but just within sight.

I thought of the friends I'd made during my rehabilitation, and how our challenges and achievements are all so different – how others' versions of my Himalaya might involve peeling a banana, getting on a motorbike again, or getting to the local shop. I realized that successfully cycling through the Himalaya had injected into me a belief that I could achieve things I had thought beyond my grasp. With some perseverance and passion for our goal, we had achieved something that most, including ourselves at times, had thought impossible. For this, I felt as strong as a mountain.

I recalled all the comments thrown at us whilst planning the trip..."Its impossible", "You won't get across that border without the support of an expedition organisation", "What about the altitude?", "How will you go to the toilet?", "What if one of you has an accident or a medical emergency"... which could have become boulders in our path, too large to negotiate. Listening to these cautious voices I had thought to myself "How? How are we ever going to manage it?" But the process of getting to the Himalaya surprised me and showed me that if we make the choice to go for something, if we say to ourselves "I'm going to do it", then it is incredible what unfolds once we make that commitment. I had wanted to experience the Himalaya on a bike so badly that despite the doubts and fears we'd been able to stay focused towards that goal.

It was as if, in making the decision to get ourselves and our bikes to Central Asia, all manner of unexpected things unfolded and occurred to help us along the way. It was only when we felt indecisive about something, or let the doubtful voices rule for a while, that we were held back from forging towards our plan. I learnt that if we want something enough, and focus our energies and efforts towards it, we will be surprised by what becomes possible. Sitting on the roof of the world in all the glory of the giant mountains, I thought "Wow! We made it". I appreciated intensely the place we were in and all that we'd had to do to get there.

Each time I tackle a new goal or challenge, I go through this same process that I first noticed through the process of getting to the high point of the Himalaya.

How? How am I ever going to manage something?

Now. I decide, despite the doubts and fears in my mind that I will try.

Wow! I've done the thing I thought I couldn't, and in doing so, I've got to know myself and the world a little better. And I feel elated, alive and free.

Whatever form our goal might take, however huge or small it may seem to others, it is reaching for those 'almost impossible' things we dream of that helps us discover ourselves.

CHAPTER 9

TRANSITION

"Sell your cleverness and buy bewilderment"
JALAL-UDDIN RUMI

Having reached the mountains that I had so long wanted to visit, I returned to Scotland and began a new career working as a geologist in the oil industry. I was carried along on the wave of starting a 'proper' job and adjusting to the demands that came with it in contrast to a less-pressured student life. It was a busy time. There wasn't much chance in the day to breathe in between long working hours, time with friends and trying to stay fit, active and healthy. Like many of us, I felt pulled in many directions.

Falling had been a feature in my life for the previous years. I had been on a quest to find ways back to mountains, and it seemed that finally I had found the means and the confidence to get there. It had been a very 'physical' three years since my fall. I had been constantly active, searching, trying, testing, eager to find ways to spend time in the wilderness that I missed so much. Eventually, I had managed to find some measure of 'normality' with all of that again, although I still lamented the peaks that I couldn't reach.

There is a part of me that has always longed for physical

adventure and journeys in the wilderness. Someone asked me "Why do you like cycling for hours, days and months? It's like you're searching for a missing piece of a jigsaw puzzle. What are you searching for?" At first I brushed the questions off, refusing to look beyond the attractions of the external world, which rushed through my hair and under my wheels. But with time I thought long and hard about that question, and the line from a U2 song kept springing into my head, "...and I still haven't found what I'm looking for...". My love of physical journeys in the wilderness is in part because it gives me a sense of freedom that I feel is sometimes limited by the physical limitations of being paralysed.

Becoming paralysed has forced me to appreciate just what freedom means to me, the value of freedom of movement and expression particularly, and to appreciate how much I'd taken it for granted. The freedom to move is something I'd never thought about or realised the importance of until it was gone. For a while, I'd been full of awe and envy just watching people move. Doing sports, and being outside, helped to alleviate any restrictions I felt.

Morning mist over the Alps, ascending Mont Blanc, July 1991

But beyond the sense of freedom, a big part of me enjoys the stimulation I get from journeys and the things that I discover about myself, other people, the world, and those unanswerable questions. Maybe my enjoyment of journeys stems from the purpose that arrives with each day, the focus that is required, the feeling of togetherness with my companions and the strength of the bonds developed in going through intense experiences. The physical journeys act as a catalyst for the journey I experience inside. So what was I looking for? I didn't know. And I didn't think I'd found it.

Something about what I'd been shunted up against made me question existence, transcendence, meaning, the greater picture of humanity. Like so many of us dealing with major change or trauma, I began to question and search. It wasn't a conscious decision, but a part of me felt that there was more to the world than I'd previously thought, and wanted to explore that. Some part of me had been awoken to believing in more than I could see.

In the past I saw the world in black and white, but something about my experiences from being paralysed had changed me, and I was beginning to see the world through different glasses. I saw it now in a spectrum of colours and shades, richer and more diverse than even a woodland in bright autumn sunshine. Now I had come to see that nothing is as 'absolute' as I'd thought it was. Nothing is a given. Nothing is forever. Change is inevitable.

It seems that one minute I was an average just-gone teenager, with a science degree and a bug for climbing, a loving family and some great friends. But I'd had a filter on the world that only believed what had been 'proven' and that what we see is what there is. Then suddenly, in a period of months and being faced with major challenges, I felt like I was twenty-one going on a hundred, with a very different view of the world. Despite three years of trying to rebuild what had been shattered, I now had so many more questions than answers, and with a sense and thirst for something unknown, mysterious, intriguing.

This is where my story turns a corner. From sharing my story of becoming paralysed, it becomes an exploration and a journey of discovery, in search of answers about existence and meaning. Alongside my very 'normal' life working as a geologist, attending an office from early until late, five days a week, emerged another entirely contrasting series of experiences, which led me into a very different river of thinking.

I recall the ideas of a friend who had discovered a belief in the existence of souls and spirits. His stories of speaking and receiving messages from spirit guides, angels, and dead relatives just didn't make sense to me. I believed in what I could see, and back then, that didn't include any ghosts or mysterious presence.

As a scientist, I believed in Darwin's theories, in evolution, in the Big Bang, in logical explanations for the world, the universe and humanity. But I've come to realize that these things are not so far removed from what might be called 'the supernatural'. Maybe 'supernatural' just means we don't quite understand it or have an explanation for it yet. I think quantum physics is starting to bridge that gap. But at this point, my journey led me in a new direction, which I could never have anticipated.

CHAPTER 10

GOLDEN MAGIC

"When one door closes another opens. Expect that new door to reveal even greater wonders and glories and surprises. Feel yourself grow with every experience. And look for the reason for it." EILEEN CADDY

L eemac was the instigator of my curious new journey. I met her at a "Fundraising Skills" night class, where I was learning how to raise money for Scotland's Alternative Skiers, eager to enable other people in my situation to enjoy the same liberating mountain experiences that I had.

Leemac seemed fascinated by the fact that I was studying for a PhD in Geology and working with Bolivian gold deposits. She was apparently eager to come and see the rock samples I had gathered from Bolivian fieldtrips. Her interest, she revealed, lay in her skill for somehow detecting precious metals by sensing their different energies. Her description didn't make much sense to me but reminded me of stories about people dowsing for water or oil. As she spoke, I couldn't suppress a creeping cynicism, but I was happy for her to come and see the rocks and learn more about what she said.

Leemac didn't wear floaty skirts, or have long hair, or smell of patchouli oil, or show any of the stereotypical characteristics I might have associated with someone who proclaimed to 'work with energies'. She dressed as a businesswoman, in crisp and stylish black suits with white ruffled blouses and she worked for a large financial institution. She spoke confidently, clearly and boldly, but her face wasn't in the least bit hard. Her skin glowed and looked softer than down, and her smile creased gently out to her ears and temples. She radiated warmth and kindness. I looked forward to our exchange.

A few weeks later, her hands hovered above a row of thirty dusty Bolivian rock samples, lined up on a laboratory bench at Aberdeen University's Geology Department. Leemac stood, smart and focused, and began to run her hand back and forth along the row of rocks. She started to shuffle them into different positions. Initially, she seemed sure of herself, and explained that she could 'feel' how much gold was in each rock. She was arranging them in order, from highest gold content to lowest. This might have been an easy task if the gold appeared as obvious nuggets within the rocks. But these particular rocks, red, orange and dusty, just looked like tired artefacts of a dry place, with no sign of any sparkling gems within them. The gold, according to my research so far, formed tiny particles locked into the lattice of minerals in the rocks.

After five or ten minutes, Leemac's rock shuffling slowed and her expression was puzzled.

"I'm not sure about these last few samples. It's hard for me to tell what order to put them in. I don't think any of them have very much gold."

She finished, and I recorded the order in which she'd placed the rocks.

"So, have you got any results for these rocks yet?" she asked.

"No. I'll get to work in the lab this week and do some analyses. Then we can see how the lab results compare with yours!"

She smiled a warm smile. When Leemac smiled, she radiated a sense that there was much more going on in her mind than she gave away. Sometimes I had the feeling that she avoided saying or attempting to explain some things, as if she thought it would sound too absurd for anyone to make sense of. As if she wanted to avoid being judged, or thought of as strange. I got the impression that she saw the world in an entirely different way from most.

A few weeks of laboratory work later, I started to understand the origins of the saying 'laborious process'. Taking each sample, crushing it up, carefully weighing out micrograms of rock powder and extracting the gold into solution took hours of patience. It

involved nasty acids, noxious fumes, protective clothing and a lot of care not to dissolve a chunk of my thigh.

Finally I was ready to run the resulting pale yellow solutions through the 'big white box', otherwise known as an 'Atomic Absorption Spectrometer', which would magically give me the gold levels in each rock sample as a

On geology fieldwork, Bolivian measurement of 'parts per million'
Andes, spring 1995 (ppm). I watched the small cups of

solution march into the machine, and as the results were delivered, I compared the quantity of gold in each sample to Leemac's ordered list.

I was amazed!

There was a near perfect match. When the rocks had less than 1ppm, the correlation diminished, but this coincided with her uncertainty about the last few samples that she didn't think contained much gold. I was very surprised, forced to surrender my cynicism, and acknowledge that she did indeed seem to have a remarkable skill.

I shared the results with my research supervisor. I knew that he had experiences in water dowsing, but watched him raise a suspicious eyebrow as I explained what had happened.

"I tell you what. Get five jars. Fill them with sand and hide a gold ring in one of them. See if she can tell which jar it's in. That should be interesting."

I duly did this, and sure enough, Leemac got it right each time. Her undeniable results were the first chink in my rigid 'scientific' belief system. What she was doing didn't fit with what I believed was possible. Yet I couldn't deny that she could quite accurately detect the gold. It seemed like magic.

Leemac explained the other aspects of her work with energies. She said that just as she could detect the vibrational energies of the gold, she could feel the energies of disease or illness, and work to improve it. She helped people with all sorts of health problems, from blood poisoning to cancer. As we spoke, she placed one of her hands over my back, above the area of my spine that was damaged. Intriguing expressions wandered over her face, and I felt a strange tingling sensation and heat beneath her hand. She asked if I would be interested in her doing some 'work' on my spinal cord. I was interested enough to agree.

The gravel of the driveway crunched beneath my wheels and I negotiated the short wooden ramp into Leemac's home. I entered a small pink room, busy with scatter cushions, a lace-clothed table and baskets of colourful rocks. She had a fascinating collection of giant crystals. I couldn't help but be attracted to their rich colours and angular forms, the geologist in me fascinated to know where she had found them all. Soft light filled the room with a glow and I followed Leemac's request to lie down on a pink silky sheet that lay on the floor. From the corner of the room, she pulled out a faded yellow washing-up bowl filled with giant quartz crystals.

"Great amplifiers for energy", she said passionately.

I was mesmerized by their clean sparkling faces, their sharp edges and the rainbow colours they projected in the light. I felt calm and relaxed, and I let my eyes close as she began to place her hands in different positions on or near my body, and moved the giant crystals into different locations on the floor immediately around me.

The cynical voice within me whispered "What is she doing?" yet the open part of me said, "Just relax and see what happens". I sank into a depth of relaxation I rarely experienced, and found myself in an imaginary land with, like a scene from a science-fiction film. I walked across moorlands of translucent crystal with giant pink and white crystalline towers on the horizon. I sat down on crystal rocks and felt the sun on my face. I felt blanketed in warmth.

Suddenly I felt irate, as if a dark cloud had just moved over and blocked out the light. My skin felt hypersensitive, and extremely uncomfortable. My consciousness shifted and I arrived back in the room.

"What did you just do?" I inquired

"I moved this crystal beside your head."

"It suddenly felt awful. Can you move it away again?"

As soon as she moved it, I felt better and was able to relax once more.

I found it difficult to comprehend how a bunch of crystals being moved around me could make me feel so good, or so bad, but my interest was captivated enough to want to experience it again. Leemac began working with me regularly, exploring the energies around my spine.

Whilst I was discovering Leemac's healing skills, my thirst for 'answers to the unknown' led me to visit the spiritualist centre in Aberdeen. I thought it would be interesting to check out what was going on there. I'd heard that they ran a course "Introduction to Spiritualism" which I thought might be as good a place as any to begin looking for answers to all of the questions that were constantly popping into my head.

I drove to Aberdeen's Dee Street on a dark winter evening, my mind fogged with nervousness like the night was with cloud. I was overflowing with apprehension, and had no idea what a "spiritualist centre" would look like. I wheeled up and down the car-lined street, granite houses stacked against each other, a cosy glow in their windows. I had no address for the centre, so I scanned the street for the most likely building.

There were small cottages, and larger houses, some of them with brass plaques outside which I peered at for clues, but they were mostly solicitors and lawyers offices. Then I saw a church-like building with a black iron sign hanging from its front, and crossed the street towards it, disappointed to see a flight of stone steps disappearing into the shadowed alcove of the entrance. "This must be it" I thought.

As I got close, I found a man dressed in a smart black suit and crisp white shirt, standing on the steps with an air of waiting. I opened my mouth to speak "Is this the spiri ...' my voice tailed off as a woman in a revealing dress clicked out of the entrance, jewellery glinting at her neck, her voice laughing "Goodnight".

I stopped myself from blurting any more words, and tried again "Excuse me, what is this building?"

"The Ministry of Sin nightclub. Not sure how to get you in here, there's steps everywhere."

"Errrmm" I stuttered with embarrassment. "It's okay. I'm looking for somewhere else". I scooted out of there as fast as I could, relieved that I hadn't asked the bouncer if it was the spiritualist centre, and laughing at how embarrassed I could have been!

I eventually found what I was looking for. It was a very innocuous building that just looked like someone's home. No one was wearing black cloaks or chanting around ouiji boards – such were my prejudiced beliefs.

I went along quite a few times to the introductory classes, where we discussed our beliefs and the possibility of a spirit world. We watched and experienced mediums at work, channelling messages from spirits. It was fascinating, interesting, vaguely con-vincing, and gave me enough 'food' to taste and chew over in relation to my questions.

I considered the possibility that there are parallel 'worlds' around us, but never received any messages from Will or anyone else, which left me slightly disappointed. I was reasonably convinced that there was something 'real' going on given the apparent accuracy of the messages other people were receiving. But I decided not to pursue it any further. I didn't feel I needed to know about the spirit world. I was too interested and engaged with the world I was in.

And beyond the healing sessions with Leemac and the others, I didn't have much emotional energy left to expend and explore elsewhere.

CHAPTER 11

GETTING LOST

*"From time without beginning, the tree of unknowing has
been watered by the monsoon of mental habit.
What a tangle of delusion it has become.
Listen. Ponder. Practice. Chop it down with the axe of the
guru's instruction."*

CAURANGIPA

E ach time I met with Leemac and the small group of others that
she had gathered and motivated to work with me, I struggled
to understand how an hour of work a couple of times a week could
really be helping with an issue as enormous as paralysis. But I
could hardly refuse the opportunity to try when the possible prize
was the most giant pot of gold that anyone could entice me with! I
focused harder than ever during the work with her. I was convinced
that Leemac had a special skill and that it could help with many
illnesses or medical problems. I was committed enough, or
attracted enough to the idea of walking again, to get myself to the
sessions even when they were arranged at extreme times of day,
from seven in the morning to ten at night.

I experienced sensations like nothing I had felt before.
Anticipation flooded through me as tingles crept, then surged,

through nerves I'd forgotten existed. Leemac explained to me that my cells had a memory, and that they could remember what it was like to move, and to walk. She said that she was working to stimulate this cellular memory. She was interested to see if it might be possible to re-establish some sensation or movement in my body. It all felt like a bizarre mystery. At times I had powerful visions of my spine as a bundle of electric cables, of colours shooting through my head and down my back, and an almost explosive sense of potential. But mostly, I was confused by the whole thing and felt emotionally fragile.

How could I possibly think, when all the scientists and doctors in the world couldn't heal a cut of the spinal cord and put an end to paralysis, that we, with nothing but tingling sensations and a sense of energy, could get me to walk? It defied logic. It seemed ridiculous. Every ounce of my scientific training told me it was impossible. But somewhere very deep inside, I wondered if the logic to which I was glued might actually be wrong.

Leemac and her ability to douse for precious metals, her work with healing energies, my experiences at the spiritual centre...all these things were starting to add up to something more than I was quite ready to accept. I had been open and questioning enough to find these things, but now I realized how much they challenged some deep-rooted beliefs that I held about the world. About what was possible and what wasn't.

A part of me was attached to logic, trusting only what I had learned, what 'fitted' with my education and experiences. That part of me led to a scepticism that spoke and fought against the dents and cracks that were beginning to appear in my 'logical' view of the world.

Contemplating, with friend Lorna Renwick whilst rowing on Loch Awe, Scotland

Leemac and the others seemed to have an absolute belief that it was possible for me to walk again. I was in awe of the pure and clear belief that seemed to shine from them. I wanted to believe it too. I imagine that anyone in a similar situation to me would want to believe the same, but maybe not everyone would begin to act on it. Being the activist that I am, and trusting the positive intentions of Leemac, I pursued the inkling of possibility that presented itself. We continued to meet on a regular basis, and with focused effort and 'channeling' of energy, our small group observed my feet and toes responding to my effort to move them – small twitches and movements which seemed to correspond with my thought and intention.

Here was a small group of people who were offering to help

me towards this enticing possibility, and I was drawn to it. A big part of me wanted to believe that I could walk again. Seeing my feet and toes move, I wanted more of it. But another part of me simply didn't think it was possible. I wondered how much of the movement was really directed by my thoughts, and how much was just involuntary movement which I knew occurred in my feet often, which happened to coincide with my intentional efforts to move them.

As the weeks went by, I realized that after each healing session, I was thrown into emotional turmoil. It was as if someone was telling me I could fly when I didn't have any wings. It was too big a leap for me to take, and I felt like a frustrated fledgling.

I tried hard to suppress the disbelieving part of me because I was scared that if I acknowledged it, I'd pollute our chances of being successful. I wanted to believe, completely, that the healing sessions could lead to the amazing result of me walking again. Yet I couldn't shake off the part of me that thought it all rather unrealistic. And the disbelieving part of me provided me with a defence, an insurance policy, that if I didn't miraculously walk, it would be okay because I hadn't invested in the concept completely.

I experienced a dilemma. I felt pressure to invest in the idea that we could heal my spinal cord. I felt that if I didn't believe wholeheartedly, with every cell of my being, that it was possible, then we would never achieve it. So I denied my uncertainty, and we continued to meet up for the healing sessions, sometimes three or four times a week. I went along, because every part of me wanted the outcome of walking. Yet I was becoming gradually more emotional about it all. I felt vulnerable.

This dilemma created a sense of unrest in me. In part I just wanted to forget about the idea of walking again and get on with life as I'd begun to know it once more. I wanted to enjoy the life where I had found a sense of balance and normality after all the upheaval. But another part of me was intrigued and excited, not only by the possibility of walking, but by the light which shone through a door that had been opened. It was a door to another world of beliefs, where I could see a sketch of meaning and purpose to life, where miracles were perhaps possible.

In some ways, the idea of walking again felt like I imagine an unwanted pregnancy might. I thought I'd let go of any attachment to walking, and felt I had moved on. But new seeds of possibility were planted and growing, disrupting the earth of stability that had settled since my accident. Like a foetus growing inside me, it wouldn't go away, and at some point, I was going to have to pay full attention to it. I tried, but just couldn't bring myself to press the 'abort and abandon' button.

In some way I think it felt naïve, like a fantasy, that together we thought we could get me to walk. I wonder how much desperation there was inside me, to get back what I had lost. I don't know any explanation for what happened during the healing sessions, but I do know that it felt quite special. I experienced very strange and unusual sensations that strengthened a belief in me about the existence of energies. In many ways it felt right and meaningful to be striving for something so extraordinary, and I wanted to believe that we could make the 'dream' come true.

Leemac and the others were warm, generous people, well-intentioned, and I was sure, skilled healers, but my engagement with them dislodged me from a place of relative acceptance with myself and being paralysed. It was six years since my accident now and I thought I'd come to accept my situation and enjoy life again. This had come along and thrown some confusion at me. That wasn't such a bad thing – it catalysed my inquiry about many of the beliefs I had held about the world. But it left me wondering whether much of what I had believed before was a delusion, or whether I was more deluded now than I had ever been!

But of course, beneath my 'veneer' of coping for the last six years, was a vulnerability about being paralysed. It had only taken Leemac to plant a seed of possibility and I was eager to explore it. Despite feeling relatively 'comfortable' about being paralysed, the adventurous part of me was bored of 'realism'. I wanted to find out where things would go. Maybe 'impossible' things could happen in the world.

As the months passed, I began to realise that I was losing myself in the whole thing. I had lost something precious to me – the ability to walk. And now I was looking to the skills of Leemac to fix me. And something about that didn't seem so healthy - there was 'neediness' in it. I was turning Leemac into the guru, feeling dependent on her knowledge, skills or power to make me better. I had lost trust in my own thoughts and feelings. She was coming from a generous and supportive place, but I was turning it into neediness because what we were doing had uncovered my vulnerability.

Looking back, it isn't at all surprising. I was under stress, my beliefs seriously challenged – I was struggling to make sense of the dichotomous worlds to which I had insight. But positively, my mind was becoming more open to possibilities, and some old probably quite unhelpful beliefs were crumbling.

CHAPTER 12

A SPIRITUAL JOURNEY

"...And I have felt
A presence that disturbs me with the joy
Of elevated thoughts; a sense sublime
Of something far more deeply interfused,
Whose dwelling is the light of setting suns,
And the round ocean and the living air,
And the blue sky, and in the mind of man:
A motion and a spirit, that impels
All thinking things, all objects of all thought,
And rolls through all things."
WILLIAM WORDSWORTH

For a while I'd been exploring other forms of complementary therapy, to aid with various physical problems I was having. Acupuncture was something I found helped me a lot, although it seemed to do more than affect me physically. Every time a needle was placed in me, I seemed to experience some kind of emotional release. It was perhaps the melting tip of the iceberg, which my emotions had largely become, resulting from all the 'staying busy', and 'must be strong' stuff that I'd done over the years.

I've always been intrigued by the twists and turns,

Sunrise over the Frontier Ridge, Mont Maudit, French Alps, August 1992

coincidences and connections that unfold in life. How one seemingly random or unimportant thing leads to a whole chain of events that eventually define the course of our life. During one incidental visit to the acupuncturist, he handed me a book called *In Search of Brazil's Quantum Surgeon*. As soon as I saw its striking cover, I was attracted to read it.

I devoured the book in one long evening, totally absorbed and fascinated by what I read.

The book was a personal account by Maki, a Japanese journalist who visited Brazil on a quest for spiritual enlightenment. The true story describes his meeting with a Brazilian computer programmer named Rubens who claimed to channel the spirit of Dr Fritz, a German First World War surgeon.

Maki visited the clinic where Dr Fritz works his miracles, appearing to heal over a thousand people a day with psychic injections and dramatic displays of near bloodless surgery. All this was apparently performed with un-sterilized surgical instruments and without anesthesia. The book was filled with stories and descriptions from qualified doctors who'd witnessed 'miracles', and there was even a mention of Dr Fritz suggesting he could help Christopher Reeve (Superman) with his spinal cord injury.

The story drew me in. I was fascinated by it, for reasons that are obvious now. It fed the part of me that wanted to believe that walking again after a severed spinal cord was possible. The book reinforced the suggestion that paralysis was something that could be healed and overcome. The door of light and intrigue that Leemac's work had opened in me, was suddenly forced wider and was beckoning me to step through it and discover what hid beyond. I had been living with the sense of tension or stress for a while, created by holding these two seemingly opposing views of the world – the left-brained logical view or the more right-brained, intuitive one that wanted to believe in miracles. I didn't want to stay in that place, with that tension. I was looking for some answers or some resolution that would help me chose one view over the other. Here was something that seemed to offer a pathway towards that.

I found an email address in the back of the book for a North American film-maker who'd spent many years researching Dr Fritz and making a film about him. In my rush of enthusiasm after reading the book, I emailed him. To my surprise, he responded immediately. His message said that a group of Americans were going to Rio to spend a week with Dr Fritz, observing and learning about his work. Many of the group would be doctors or consultants who had a particular interest in alternative forms of medicine and healing. I instantly wanted to join them. I had annual leave to spare and with four years of working behind me, some small savings.

Within a few days, I was signed up to join their group. It seemed a coincidence that British Airways flights to Rio were on special offer, which added force to my decision to go. I would go to Rio for ten days, in ten days time.

Over the next days, my stomach was like cappuccino – all the froth of anxiety and doubt with sprinkles of excitement. The equivalent of the coffee hit would be arriving in Brazil, and part of me expected that I would find it a shock.

I started to wonder and worry what I was letting myself in for. I pulled an old book off my shelf. It was called *Spiritual Healing – Miracle or Mirage?* I had been given it several years ago but at the time, its words might as well have been in Russian for all I could understand of it. But now I pulled its blue shiny cover from the shelf and flicked to the contents page. A name leapt out at me. There, in black and white on a book I'd had for years was a section on Dr Fritz! He was featured in a chapter about spirit doctors. I felt that it was a sign that I was doing the right thing. Then I wondered, "When did I start believing in 'signs'?"

I told nobody except my house mates and a close friend where I was going. I was in some ways embarrassed to admit the truth behind my visit to Brazil. I saw something crazy in me trying to explain, "I read a book about this spirit surgeon and I thought I'd go and see all about it for myself. And maybe I'll get to walk again too …". I thought friends might judge me and think, "She's finally lost the plot". I didn't want to have to get involved in long conversations or judgements about the book, the story or my reasons for going. I didn't want to worry anybody at home. It was something I just felt compelled to do, and a journey that I wanted to make alone.

The night before flying to Brazil, I lay on a crisp bed in a sterile hotel room, the froth in my stomach foaming out of control.

"What am I doing?" I asked myself.

I seriously questioned my sanity for flying halfway around the globe to see some weird spirit surgeon. But I was already on my way, and my curiosity wouldn't let fear or doubt stop the adventure.

My head rolled lazily on the starchy pillow and I noticed a red hardback Bible on the bedside table. I didn't know the Bible beyond a distant memory of some childhood Sunday School classes, but now I reached to pick it up. I randomly opened it in the middle, and read.

"...Some men came carrying a paralysed man on a mat and tried to take him into the house to lay him before Jesus. When they could not find a way to do this because of the crowd, they went up on the roof and lowered him on his mat through the tiles into the middle of the crowd, right in front of Jesus.

When Jesus saw their faith, he said, "Friend, your sins are forgiven."

The Pharisees and the teachers of the law began thinking to themselves, "Who is this fellow who speaks blasphemy? Who can forgive sins but God alone?"

Jesus knew what they were thinking and asked, "Why are you thinking these things in your hearts? Which is easier: to say, 'Your sins are forgiven,' or to say, 'Get up and walk'? But that you may know that the Son of Man has authority on earth to forgive sins..." He said to the paralysed man, "I tell you, get up, take your mat and go home." Immediately he stood up in front of them, took what he had been lying on and went home praising God. Everyone was amazed and gave praise to God. They were filled with awe and said "We have seen remarkable things today."…"

I felt like someone had just punched me between the eyes. Of all the things I could have read from the Bible's thick text, this paragraph just seemed too pertinent. I made a mental note that it was *Luke 5:17*. I quietly closed the cover and put it back on the bedside table, a little shaken by the strangeness of reading that specific passage. "Was it another sign?" I wondered again. "And if so, where are these signs coming from? Or am I just imagining it? Am I going nuts?"

I went back to the time after Scott's fall and Will's death and remembered the sensation I'd had that something, an external force, had some influence over what happens in our lives. I felt again that I was on a journey that I didn't have complete control over. I definitely had choices about what to do. I was in full control about whether or not I went to Brazil. But it seemed that if I were to be true to the 'signs' that seemed to be presenting themselves, then actually I had to go.

What did these 'signs' mean, or was I just imagining it all? Were they coming from within me, around me, 'above' me? Was there a greater force or energy in operation here? Was that what people call God?

At that thought, I almost felt a sense of dread. It had always felt easier to hold religion at arm's length. I didn't know if God existed, and in the past I hadn't cared to speak about such intangible concepts. I didn't see the point in mulling over something that I would probably never find an answer to. God fell into that realm that wasn't black and white. I was a scientist at heart, or so I had thought, and more interested in concrete 'data'. I had better things to do with my Sundays than go to church and hail praise to a concept that I couldn't grasp. The ritual and ceremony held no attraction. So, on the whole, I'd shied away from religion and any ideas of God. And now I felt wary of what I was beginning to explore.

I had thought in the past that religion acts like a crutch to people in times of difficulty. It seemed to offer a harbour from stormy waters, but one which I'd never cared to moor my boat in. I wondered about its attraction to people in vulnerable or lonely positions. I'd already discovered my vulnerability, and handed my trust over once before, and in doing so lost trust in myself. I didn't want to do that again, not to anyone, nor to the powerful umbrella of religion. I felt open yet somewhat guarded.

But it seemed churlish to run away. How could I ignore something that people fought wars over? Why would I want to dismiss a topic that is the core of so much in the world? Why had I always connected God with religion? Religions just provide structures of beliefs at which God, or a collection of Gods, is the core. But maybe the concept of God didn't need to be tied so tightly to any religion. Suddenly, I was absorbed, and there seemed nothing more important than exploring these questions.

I slept restlessly. I was disturbed by questions and more questions.

CHAPTER 13

CHALLENGING BELIEFS

*"When the heart weeps for what it has lost, the spirit
laughs for what it has found."*
SUFI APHORISM

The sun felt hot and piercing to my bleached winter pallor. I
realized that my skin was even whiter than the sand. The surf,
a washing powder glow and a roar of tumbling foam, competed in
volume with the strings of traffic filing along the seafront strip.
Semi-naked bodies and an array of colours paraded the beach.
There were lots of smiling, happy people. A surfboard passed by,
almost obscuring its sculptured owner with his bronzed shining
muscles.

Out in the bay, lumps of tree-coated rock rose from the
emerald sea. My eyes felt heavy with the remnants of jet lag as I
lazily observed the coastal scene. It was almost exactly as I'd
pictured it. I drank coconut milk direct from its hairy shell. There
I was, at Copacabana Beach, Rio de Janiero.

A few days previously I had been studying the physics of
rocks, and now there I was, in pursuit of a deceased German spirit
doctor. It seemed a startling contradiction. How on earth had I
brought myself here on the basis of a book about a dead doctor?

Intrigue, cheap flights to Rio, and holiday to spare. Why not? I answered my own question, but I knew there was more to it than that.

I picked the book up again, and flicked back through its pages as I sipped my coconut milk. I re-read the part where Fritz said he thought he could help Christopher Reeve.

"In this case, Mr. Reeve injured the spinal nerve very badly, so it is impossible for a complete cure. But I can make him well enough to be able to walk with a crutch...I would need to remove the titanium and rejuvenate the bone in the spinal cord."

It was the autumn of the millennium, almost eight years now since I'd last walked, and the prospect of it, even with a crutch, held me in awe.

I'd unconsciously censored admitting to my compelling reasons for coming to Brazil. There was a jewel of hope hiding in my heart. What if Dr Fritz really could heal a spinal cord? He certainly seemed to have a track record of success.

I'd had all sorts of silent conversations with my subconscious. I'd reasoned that at worst this whole experience would be an unusual holiday in Brazil. At best, I'd dared to imagine myself leaping with wild ecstasy in the waves, my wheelchair abandoned for a rediscovered freedom.

If I'd read Maki's book a few years previously, I would have dismissed it as a case of imagination gone wild. Accepting the possibility of spirits and unexplained healing with bloodless, painless, non-sterile, anaesthesia-free surgery would have clashed with my beliefs about the world and been too 'way out' for me to even give the time of day.

Isn't it strange, how we can be so much in denial? The

existence of other ways of seeing can stare us in the face. Yet if they conflict with our beliefs too harshly, our subconscious fear of our world being rocked can lead us to ignore and delete the information from our minds. Why do we need to think in such 'concrete' terms about the world? What does it take to wake us up?

It seemed that I'd had to fall off a cliff and smash up my body to begin waking up. I'd obviously needed a big jolt.

I left the beach in search of a room for the night. I wandered the busy streets behind the promenade area, following the directions of a guidebook to a hostel. I knew it wouldn't be easy to find an affordable place that was free of steps and narrow doorways. I pulled back the creaky iron gate that led to the hostel, and at the sight of a flight of stairs to the front door, groaned inside. The owner came down to greet me, and noticed my disappointed expression. She smiled softly, and with my broken Spanish I understood some of her fluent Portuguese. It went something like "Don't worry, follow me".

She led me to the back of the house, where she hollered for some help and flung open a dark wooden door. Inside was a garage filled with bunk beds. A sun-withered man arrived on the scene. He started shifting the beds and furniture around so that I could get into the cluttered space. They smiled satisfied grins at me, patted some blankets and left me alone.

In the musty garage buried in the back streets, I threw its heavy doors open to cast some light into the gloomy windowless interior and inspected my new abode.

Five sets of bunk beds and some old green lockers had been crammed haphazardly into the space. The mattresses were covered in brown vinyl, sticky and squeaky in the heat. A strip of mosaic-patterned lino had been stuck badly along the centre of the stained concrete floor, rippled and bumpy beneath my wheels. The air smelt stale and heavy.

The garage doors opened onto a long gated driveway, and beyond, a jumble of concrete blocks of all shapes and sizes rambled over the hillside that climbed steeply to a rich blue sky at its crest. Dense tropical vegetation filled the gaps between the buildings. Mazes of wire tangled through the trees. I felt very alone in the urban jungle. I felt almost crazy. I wished I had a friend there to talk with, to share it all with, to help make sense of things. I felt intensely paranoid and nervous of what I was entering into.

The next day, I would meet with the American group at the airport, along with Rubens – whose body Dr Fritz possessed. Maybe it would all seem more real and rational when thirteen other people arrived here for the same reason. Alongside my fear was excitement. I was fearful of wanting to walk again in case of disappointment. I had a curious duality of belief and disbelief, excitement and fear within me.

I reminded myself how much being here seemed to have been led by a series of 'coincidences', the succession of signs that had compelled me to come here. Whatever transpired, I just had to trust that I was in the right place, and make the most of it.

I tossed and turned through a restless night of sleep and woke to rays of sun that seeped through the cracks in the wooden door. It was time to leave the dingy garage and start the adventure in full.

I somehow negotiated the steps of a spluttering bus, which I flagged down on the Copacabana strip, and on my way to the airport, gazed at the sea and sprawling favellas through its dirty windows. I waited at the arrivals gate to meet the flight from

Orlando on which the others were due. Loud floral shirts and an array of hats paraded past me. Finally, one of the passengers, smiling broadly, asked with a heavy accent,

"Are you Karen?"

I smiled back, and was rapidly introduced to the colourful group. Intense talk was mixed with jet-lagged silence as we drove through the busy Rio suburbia to our hotel. It was a glamorous word for a long corridor of very simple rooms attached to a quiet convent clinging to a steep hillside. This would be our home for the next week.

I was glad to be with other people to talk to about why we were there, rather than going in circles with my own thoughts.

Over dinner that evening, any doubt about why I'd come dissolved whilst Bruce (Doctor Rind) described some of his previous 'Fritz experiences' to me.

"I was down here two years ago, and followed Fritz for a day. He treated around 1000 patients. I couldn't keep up with him! I saw amazing things. Eyeballs popped out and cut, replaced, and blindness cured. I watched a paraplegic man stand and walk. He was operated on three weeks previously, and in this time, regained some movement in his legs. He showed me his small leg movements, and then Fritz operated on his back again. I didn't really see, as I was too engrossed in watching a brain tumour being removed. But then I felt a tap on my shoulder, and this paraplegic Brazilian guy was standing beside me. Well I guess he wasn't paraplegic anymore. He'd just left his wheelchair and walked. His muscles were still completely atrophic, but it didn't seem to matter. He was walking normally. It was as if he was a normal individual just getting used to his legs after sitting around for a long time."

My heart leapt.

"Later I got talking to a girl in a wheelchair who'd had some other treatments. I told her about the astonishing thing that I'd witnessed. She previously hadn't thought of asking Fritz to do 'the impossible', but now she went to him and asked. Then I saw her crying and leaving. He'd told her he couldn't help as her spinal cord was totally severed."

My heart dived. I believed from doctors at home that my cord was completely severed.

Bruce smiled at me, "I hope he can help you."

That night, lying in the simple room with only a crucifix decorating the blue painted walls, I read more about the history of Dr Fritz in some books lent to me by one of the Americans.

In the 1950s, an uneducated Catholic farm boy named Ze Arigo began to fall into involuntary, violent trance states in which he would mumble in what seemed to be a foreign language. He was treated by doctors, who found nothing physically wrong, and by a priest who unsuccessfully tried to exorcise the demon from him. However, it was no demon, but the spirit of Dr Adolf Fritz, a German doctor who had died in World War I, and now was insisting that Arigo start healing the sick. At first, the cures were simple prescriptions that functioned to alleviate many of the town people's illnesses, but one night Dr Fritz, through the unconscious body of Arigo, performed a surgery on a good friend and well-known Senator to remove a cancerous tumour from his lung. When the Senator returned to his doctor, who pronounced him healed by the extraordinary surgery, the Senator announced to the press this remarkable story and Arigo's fame spread like wild-fire.

Over twenty years he and Dr Fritz treated an estimated two million people from all over the world, whilst suffering from the constant pressure of the law, Church and medical associations infuriated with his unorthodox healings. Support from powerful individuals like the Brazilian president, whose daughter he treated, and American scientists who could vouch for his authenticity, offered the chance for him to be able to continue healing until his sudden death in a car crash in 1971.

Dr Frtiz had apparently appeared in other mediums over the following years, the most well-known being Edson Queiroz, advancing the techniques of Arigo to include the use of needles. Like his predecessor, he suffered a violent death at a fairly young age.

Rubens Faria, who currently channels Dr Fritz, was born in Sao Paulo in 1954, and graduated as a telecommunications engineer. He has no medical background. Dr Fritz, however, commands a vast knowledge of physiology, anatomy, nuclear medicine, quantum mechanics, and healing of the astral body. Rubens is under constant pressure from the medical association in Brazil for illegal practice of healing and struggles to attend to seemingly unending lines of those who have been left with no hope by those same medical professionals. To cover costs, he requests a small donation from those who can afford it. For others, he purchases medicines, bus fares and even donates food. Fortunately, Dr Fritz has valuable support from certain doctors who have been cured by him and who now donate their time assisting with surgeries.

It was a fascinating story. I remembered my conversation with a surf-rescue guy just a few days ago at the beach. He had asked me what I was doing in Brazil and I'd replied that I was here to visit a special surgeon who had a reputation for amazing healings. He immediately said "Oh, Dr Fritz?" I was surprised. "Yeah, he does some extraordinary things. He is famous here in Brazil. Good luck, I hope he can help you." Clearly Dr Fritz was well known and, it seemed, respected in Brazil. I was reminded again of how we live with such diverse realities.

The next morning, we gathered in a spacious room with bare stone walls and sweeping curves shaping its grandiose roof.

Before Rubens arrived, Tom, who had organized the trip, showed us a video of his own surgery in 1997. He had a neck problem after an accident had left him with a lot of pain and nerve damage. Dr Fritz had taken a circular electric saw to his neck! Tom told us he had felt nothing, though when he'd heard the saw and smelt burning bone, he had felt repulsed at the thought of what was happening. A few weeks later his neck was perfectly recovered. Apparently, Dr Fritz works with a team of medical specialists on the spiritual plane, such as an orthopaedist and an anaesthesiologist, who participate in the diagnosis and treatment of the many types of ailments. Tom's surgery was largely due to the assistance of another surgeon who Fritz referred to as Ricardo, who apparently enjoyed the drama of electric tools.

Regardless of the explanation, I was amazed at the sight of an electric circular saw being taken to someone's neck, at the apparent absence of pain without drugs, and at the curious lack of blood. As I watched the video, I hoped there would be no electric saws around that week.

Rubens' arrival broke our collection of gaping jaws. He had a kind face with a smile that radiated calm and sensitivity. He had a modest character, and warmly said hello to each of us individually, shaking hands and kissing cheeks. We rearranged our seats in a semi-circle around him, and then fell quiet as Rubens sat, closed his eyes for a few minutes, and 'left' to be replaced by Dr Fritz.

Fritz's guttural voice and sparkling eyes, very different to those of Rubens, broke the silence. It was odd, to see the same body, and the same features, but to have a sense that indeed, this was a completely different person. His facial expressions, his sense of humour, his mannerisms and tone of voice were all very changed. I wondered if I was imagining it, but later, everyone agreed.

Ken, a doctor from Utah, volunteered to be one of the first on the table, which, covered with a blanket and sheet, was our makeshift operating theatre. He had a pain in his neck that had bothered him for years. Dr Fritz pulled out a scalpel and began to cut the skin over the vertebrae, but the blade was blunt. There was no anaesthetic, no sterilisation, and yet no pain, and apparently no cases of infection.

He laughed and moved to the stone wall to sharpen the blade. He had an odd sense of comedy, and seemed to enjoy shocking us by adding frills like this to his performance.

He cut through to the bone, and then hammered the scalpel. The sound of striking metal was amplified by the arched roof of the room. It resounded through my own bones. We all cringed as our small group, huddled around the table, caught each other's eyes. But Ken didn't even flinch.

Then Dr Fritz turned his head and laughed again. "A church? This is a church! Ha!" It was the power of the Brazilian churches that had forced the government to make his surgeries illegal. No wonder he found it amusing.

The surgery on Ken's neck took only a few minutes. Two stitches later he was back on his feet, feeling a little tight in his neck, but otherwise with no indication that he'd just had an operation.

We witnessed two days of astonishing surgeries, none of which made any anatomical sense to our understanding of the body. The American doctors in the group – Ken, Bruce and Harold – constantly questioned Dr Fritz about his actions.

"What are you doing Dr Fritz?" Bruce asked.

"I am working on the energetic body, not the physical. Diseases are initiated by problems in the bodies not visible to you. That is what I work on."

"But why do you need to do surgeries?"

"The metal helps conduct the energy into the physical body, and accelerate healing."

Our faces were puzzled.

"Actually, there is no necessity for any surgical procedures, but when I perform these visible cuts, the patient can see and truly believe that he has received a cure. I heal through the application of energy on the astral body, which is like a template that surrounds the physical body. The astral body then reflects this healthy energy into reforming diseased bodily tissues and structures."

Dr Fritz kept looking at me, his eyes piercing deep into my body. It was as if he had X-ray eyesight and was scanning me with his eyes. His eyes were kind though, not spooky in any way, and he kept smiling at me and tickling my ear.

"Ready? I would like to have a closer look at you," Fritz

spoke to me.

"Okay." Inside my stomach fluttered.

A few of the group helped me onto the table. I laid on my front whilst he scanned me more closely and then Ken, Bruce and Harold asked questions.

"If the spinal cord is cut, I cannot, unfortunately, help." My flutters turned to churning.

"But in your case, I can help. Your nerves are not completely cut."

I held my breath. I hardly dared to ask my burning question, but he read my mind.

"You will be able to walk a little, but first I need to do surgery. Today I will prepare you. Tomorrow I will operate."

I couldn't see or feel anything he was doing. I just laid there with my mind spinning and my face buried in a pillow.

Part of me thought it was odd that I had so willingly laid on a makeshift operating table and allowed this bizarre doctor, or engineer, or whoever he was, to inject me. That same part of me thought it even stranger that tomorrow I was seriously considering letting him tamper with my spine and carry out surgery. What was he really doing? Didn't I want to know more about the details of the procedure and his plans before going ahead? What would the doctors at home say if I came back with a giant scar in my back? I had questions and more questions.

Yet another part of me was more than willing to go with it. That part of me was intrigued, fascinated and had seen and heard enough to convince me that it was worth a go. I questioned whether this part of me was being irrational and hasty. Was my desire to walk again making me vulnerable and over-trusting?

Later I watched a video recording of the day. Whilst I'd laid on the table, he had injected me, once in the neck and once in the thoracic region, using giant needles, about four inches long, painfully thick in appearance, and certainly not sterile. He had according to the group of doctors, used a mixture of alcohol and iodine in the injection, with a tiny amount of turpentine added to the concoction. Illogical and poisonous though it seemed to us, he apparently used this mix quite often, as he said it created a biochemical environment for destruction of infected or cancerous tissues and regeneration of healthy cells.

"This is to move the energy," he explained. It was lost on our level of understanding.

The questions in my mind felt like a giant mountain range – one that I had to find my path through before tomorrow morning! A huge chunk of me was eager to go through with the surgery, yet there was this 'doubting' voice that kept asking me questions. It felt similar to those voices of doubt and reason I'd heard so often before our adventure through the Himalaya. What if something goes wrong? Am I biting off more than I can chew? I thought how in so many of my outdoor adventures I often felt fearful. Yet more often than not, going ahead reaped enormous rewards. A view from a mountain top onto a carpet of silent clouds; a glassy calm sea mirroring the sky. Everything we do in life carries risk. But if we consider the risks, are mindful of them, and go into things with this awareness, we are less likely to be taken by surprise.

My gut feeling was to go with it. I felt an urge to stop holding onto the need for logic and explanations that I could comprehend. I realized that I would regret not going ahead with it now I had come all this way. For all that I tried to fool myself that I was in

Brazil with Dr Fritz out of natural curiosity, I knew that deep down, the hope of being operated on was the core reason why I had come. No one had talked me into this. Nobody had persuaded me to come here. I had followed my instincts across the Atlantic, and I wasn't about to run away from that instinct now.

I spent a nervous night wrestling with my single white sheet in the heat and tropical humidity. My thoughts of leaving and running away from the craziness of the situation slowly diminished. It seemed less crazy now I was here and the things I'd read about were real. My emotions were a cocktail of fear, belief, excitement, disbelief, nervousness, amazement ... I felt that I was caught in the story of a very strange dream.

Our group with Rubens Faria (Dr Fritz), outskirts of Rio de Janeiro, Brazil, October 2000

CHAPTER 14

COSMIC QUESTIONS

"Love becomes the ultimate answer to the ultimate human question."
ARCHIBALD MACLEISH

Yet all through that restless night, I knew that I was willing to let him work on me.

The next morning, I was overflowing with anticipation as we gathered around the tables, in the room that Tom had filled with a calming smell of sage. My stomach flipped as Rubens arrived and sat down to 'bring Fritz in'. Dr Fritz joined us once more and said he wanted to delay all the big surgeries until the following day. I was disappointed. I'd spent the night mentally preparing myself, and now I just wanted to do it. Or to have it done to me, whatever 'it' all was. I would have to endure another restless night.

Meanwhile, we saw more inconceivable things. Harold volunteered for eye surgery to correct his poor vision. The concept of a scalpel plunging into an organ as sensitive as the eye put fear into all of us. We watched, fascinated but strangely calm, as he pushed the scalpel into Harold's eyeball. He cut in a radial pattern around the iris. I held Harold's hand. His muscles were totally relaxed and his palm cool. It was my hand that gripped tighter as

I watched.

It was a brief operation and Dr Fritz finished with instructions to keep a gauze patch on the eye for a day, and then to wear sunglasses and avoid bright light for a week. Later, Harold told me that he had many fears in his life, and that some years ago, he'd decided that the best way to deal with them was to face them. "Eye surgery was the thing that scared me most, so I decided to do it." I was impressed. By the next morning, his distance vision was already much improved. A few days later, he asked for his other eye to be treated.

The day of the big surgeries arrived. On the list was my spinal surgery, a liver surgery on Tanya to treat her Hepatitis C, kidney surgery for cancer on Papa-San, the Japanese father-in-law of Tom, and the removal of a malignant tumour from Meredith's groin. We sat silent, anticipating the surgeries and praying in our own worlds, as Rubens 'went out' and Dr Fritz 'came in'.

I kept my eyes closed. I was nervous, yet with no doubt that I wanted to do this. I hoped though that I wouldn't be first. I opened my eyes and Dr Fritz stood before me, his eyes penetrating. I was first.

The group helped to lift me up onto the high table again and I laid on my front. Suddenly I was crying. Tears poured emotion from me in rivers. Everyone was concerned "Are you okay Karen?" but they were not tears of fear. Crying was a release and a relief. They were tears that for years I'd been hiding, behind the mask that I'd been wearing. As I lay there, I experienced how sad I really was about my loss of movement.

It was as if I could finally show and feel what I truly felt deep inside. I felt no pain as Fritz's knife penetrated through to my

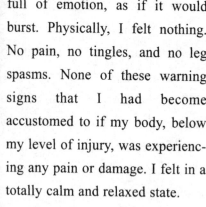

Under the rusty knife of Dr Fritz for the first time, Rio de Janeiro suburbs, October/November 2000

spine, but my heart felt huge and full of emotion, as if it would burst. Physically, I felt nothing. No pain, no tingles, and no leg spasms. None of these warning signs that I had become accustomed to if my body, below my level of injury, was experiencing any pain or damage. I felt in a totally calm and relaxed state.

As Fritz operated, he explained.

"You will experience tingling. Intense. Then strong spasm in your legs. Then you will have some pain as the nerves begin working. And small movements. Then you must fight. Do your exercises." He struggled to pronounce physiotherapy in his Germanic English. "Then you will be walking, with help. Be strong."

He left my side to operate on Papa-san. Meredith and Ken stitched me up. I needed seven stitches around my first and second lumbar vertebrae. My original injury was much higher, in my upper thoracic region, but he explained that my lower back was where the energy was blocked. My body began to tingle with discomfort as they stitched, Fritz's presence already concentrated elsewhere. Fritz came back and held Ken's hands, explaining that he was transferring energy to him so that he could stitch without causing any pain. After that, I didn't notice any sensations.

I lay recovering on a mattress on the floor of the room for a few hours. I didn't feel like I had anything physical to recover from, but it felt like the right thing to do.

The following day, we didn't have any surgeries to watch. Instead, Fritz taught to us about 'the world and the universe'. He explained that there were some key places on earth that are the focus of energy. Much like acupuncture points on the body, he explained that these were acupuncture points on earth, connecting it to the universe.

As a child I remembered lying staring at the night sky, wondering what was out there and where the earth fitted in the greater scheme of the universe. With the speed of lightning and gushing energy, Fritz scribbled mathematical and quantum-physics equations onto a blackboard, answering a stream of cosmic questions.

He explained that there were a series of energetic dimensions within the universe. Similar to the way water can turn to ice, or evaporate to steam with the application of different amounts of energy, he described how the world we knew could change to different vibrational levels. He said that the earth was currently in the 'fourth dimension' and that the human race, with our current thought patterns, were holding it back from progressing through to a new level of energetic vibration. He also stated that humans were too 'dense' in their general outlook – too focused on material possessions and power to raise the vibration to a 'lighter' level and allow the whole universe to move forward into the next energetic dimension.

In one way, what he said made a lot of sense. I liked the scientific slant that his explanations had taken, but I wasn't enough of a quantum physicist to understand the details that he scribbled before us. The gist of his message though, was very simple. He was suggesting that our thoughts influence our state of mind, and thus our feeling of 'lightness' or 'heaviness'. The 'lighter' we could become, by thinking more positively and by holding more humanistic rather than materialistic values, showing love for ourselves and each other, then the more each one of us could contribute to raising the overall vibrational energy of the earth. This would help the universe as a whole move through to another dimension.

He explained that there were twelve dimensions in total, the ultimate consisting of pure love. I got the impression that he was suggesting it was this 'final' dimension which people referred to as heaven or the meeting with God.

I was blown away by hours of explanation about the meaning of life, even though I couldn't begin to grasp the enormous scale of his theories. Although captivated and fascinated, we were struggling to understand it all and kept becoming wrapped up in complicated details. He reiterated to us the simplicity of his underlying message, "Enjoy being human, and have love in your heart, for everything and everyone".

That was the message he left us with. For all the complexity of explanation, the astounding mathematical equations that he'd scribbled before us, that was the one simple message he kept repeating.

On the plane back to Britain, I had visions of walking along a beach. My heart burst as I imagined the privilege of sensation and the return of movement. I imagined how special it would be to sense touch, to feel sand oozing through my toes, the sea lapping at my calves; to experience the pleasures of normal body functions;

to pee without a tube; to orgasm. All the things I'd taken for granted until they were gone, but as I soared through the air above the Atlantic, I imagined them so strongly that I almost believed they were real.

I told the man in the seat beside me the story. He was incredulous. He listened in disbelief. I realized from his reaction that when I got home, most people would think I was crazy as I told them what had happened to me in Brazil. The prospect of explaining to my doctor why I needed seven stitches removed from my spine preoccupied me for a while. I resolved to ask a trainee-doctor friend to remove them instead, avoiding the need for long explanations to the medical establishment.

In the scientific education that I'd received, I had been taught to question, to analyze, to look for evidence, to do experiments with repeatable results before they could be qualified. I had been conditioned by a paradigm that didn't like things that couldn't be explained logically. If there was no theory or equation to explain a phenomenon, then it couldn't be true. But now, in the face of my experiences in Brazil, none of that made sense anymore. I didn't have an explanation or proof that made any scientific sense. Yet burning inside me was a kind of proof I'd never experienced before. It was my own experience. I knew I hadn't imagined it, as I had thirteen Americans to confirm it and a video to illustrate it. But I knew in the world of science that wasn't enough to prove anything.

In Brazil, Dr Fritz and his extraordinary work was widely accepted. He apparently wasn't the only one with such skills. The people of Brazil seemed to believe in something very different to the majority of people I knew at home. They lived with a completely different picture of reality and what was possible.

As the endless azure heaven shone through the window of the plane, I wondered if I'd just experienced God. I wondered whether the meaning of life and existence was, as Fritz suggested, simply about love.

CHAPTER 15

CRUMBLED FOUNDATIONS

"The most powerful thing you can do to change the world, is to change your own beliefs about the nature of life, people, reality to something more positive ... and begin to act accordingly."

SHAKTI GAWAIN

My experiences in Brazil turned my life upside down. I was left struggling to make sense of my 'normal' life. I sat in front of the computers at work, gazing at the flickering screens, unable to focus on the tasks that pressed. Mentally and emotionally I felt like I'd been in a boxing match – punched in my head and my heart so hard that nothing I knew made sense any more. The world I had constructed around me was crumbling under the blast of this latest experience. The foundations of my world had, in that week, changed from solid rock to sand. I realized that my whole life until then had been based on an unchallenged framework of beliefs and rules that I'd been immersed in from birth. Beliefs that were derived from education, from the medical profession and from the institutions and constructs of the world around me. The evidence I had seen and experienced in Brazil challenged all of this.

The situation was intolerable. Each day I felt dazed and completely unable to focus on the daily demands. Something had to change. I felt as I had never felt before. The emotional pain of being paralysed – the loss, isolation, anger, fear – came flooding out of me. My desire to avoid these negative emotions had, in the past, been so strong that I'd just put on a brave face and immersed myself in endless activities, unconsciously avoiding the pain of loss. But now, I didn't care. I just wanted my pain gone. I wanted the nightmare to end, and Fritz's work to give me back what I had lost.

I had been fooling myself that I was okay. I thought I was fine! FINE! Fucked-up, Insecure, Neurotic and Emotional was a great definition for that word. That was exactly how I felt now. FINE!

I realized that in all the years since my accident I had just been plastering over my pain. I'd put temporary patches over my emotional black hole, sealing the edges neatly with denial, eager to bury and forget the hurt. I'd never dared to peel off the plaster and see where that black hole might take me in case the intensity of emotion that I felt was so great that I sank into depression and never recovered. I'd thought my pain was irresolvable. Nothing could bring back my uninjured body, so I might as well just grin and bear it.

Grin and bear it! Well, I had born it all right. I'd fought the pain hard and done everything in my power to avoid having to feel what was hiding within me. I'd become so good at being busy, that I didn't even realize what I was doing. I had become a master at deceiving myself. For years I had felt proud that I had never had to see a counsellor or a psychologist. I felt proud that I had been 'so strong'. I felt proud that I had done so much, and achieved so much physically.

And now, I felt a crumbling wreck. Now I realized how all of the brave face and feeling proud that I'd managed to be so emotionally independent had been a sham. It had all been my ego, desperate to appear strong.

"You're an inspiration," are words I'd often hear from others; "So brave and positive about everything". But now I realized that those words were rooted in a society conditioned to value strength. A society that values 'putting on a brave face' and coping. How many of us feel the pressure to do this when difficult things happen to us? When we fall off our summit and feel that we've sunk to the bottom of the deepest sea, how hard do we try to convince the world that we've just slipped a few steps backwards, rather than dare to share the truth and vulnerability of what we're feeling?

But something that Fritz had done or said to me had ripped off my plaster patch, and opened up my darkest hole. I was in a giant storm with tornados so powerful that I couldn't imagine how I would recover. I had lived my life valuing strength and the ability to physically do and achieve. And now, ten years after my accident, my black holes had returned to haunt me. I had to stop. Everything. I needed to give myself space to emotionally convalesce. It was a journey that would be more challenging than any physical endeavour I'd ever undertaken.

I emailed Rubens and asked him to ask Fritz about when I might expect to start feeling changes. I needed a timescale. And I needed contact, to remind myself that what I had experienced had really happened ... that I wasn't just dreaming it. Rubens replied that he was going to Hawaii, to the island of Maui for the next couple of months and that Fritz would like to do another surgery on me. I noticed the neediness in me, and realised once more that I was looking to 'the healer' to fix me. But it also felt okay – I couldn't get very dependent on someone who lived on the other side of the planet.

In the storm that I was experiencing, I needed an anchor to hold me fast. I needed to be in an environment where I could talk about it, with people who understood, believed or had experienced something similar. I emailed Ken, and he was also planning to go to Maui. In fact, five of the group that had been in Brazil lived in Maui. I decided that I would go there too. I needed to make more sense of things and in Aberdeen, faced with sceptical responses when I shared my experience and computer screens that seemed empty and bland, I just couldn't weather the storm.

My saving grace in those few weeks were my house mates. Margaret, Melissa and Laura were firm friends to me, open, supportive and solid. They were happy to talk to me about my experiences, didn't seem to think I was crazy, and didn't appear to judge me or the situation I'd got myself into. I've never thought of myself as a drama queen and generally think that I take things in my stride. But I can see how the experiences that I'd got myself into, the emotions they'd aroused, and the response that they called for, could have been perceived as somewhat dramatic. I felt like a kid on my first day at school, bursting with excitement at the encounters that lay ahead, yet scared and intimidated by the unknown.

I was anxious about taking time off work, and spent days worrying myself about what to do. But it felt so crucial to take time out and to go to Maui that I realized I was willing to give up my job to do it.

It took me a while to build up the courage to go and speak to my boss. I couldn't be bothered with lies or distortions. I just told a brief and simple account of what had happened. I asked him for unpaid leave, sure that he would think my story was crazy, and wouldn't want someone so bonkers working for the company anyway. But he took me by surprise. When I'd finished my shortened explanation, he simply looked at me and said, "There's so much more to the world than we can see. Take the time you need and we'll see you when you get back." If I'd been standing, I would have fallen over with shock.

I've found more often since then that whenever I'm honest about how I feel, the logistics seem to unexpectedly fall into place to support whatever it is I need to do to follow that truth within me. But it doesn't stop it from being scary to do so.

In the interim few weeks before I left for Maui, I joined a meditation class in Aberdeen. I had to do something to help me find a sense of calm within myself. The warmth and softness of the lady that greeted me at the door was welcoming, like finding shelter on a wet wild night. I felt comfortable entering the incense-filled, dimly lit room of the meditation centre, where a small collection of silent figures sat quietly, mostly dressed in white.

I spoke to the lady about what had happened in Brazil and what I'd been experiencing since. She shared with me the concepts behind her particular school of meditation – to focus on a bright light or object with open eyes, so that the mind could become clear.

I tried and struggled to begin with. My eyes stung within

minutes of staring at the candle. With my eyes open, I was easily distracted by objects or movements around the room. In some attempts, I fought plummeting into sleep. But I persisted and eventually, I somehow dropped into a place of quiet peace. It was as if I could watch my emotions moving through me, without feeling them in the same raw way and without becoming wrapped up in the drama of them. I was able to experience my emotions without becoming them.

After that evening, I meditated more often. I enjoyed watching my feelings, acknowledging them and allowing them to flow through my body as a river flows through the mountains. I watched them twisting and bubbling, changing direction and tempo.

If we dam a river, the water backs up. I thought how for years, I had tried so hard to dam my emotions, to control them and almost pretend they weren't there. Just as a dam, if left for long enough, builds pressure and starts leaking, my emotions had slowly leaked through. They had gradually been eating at the cracks in my dam's plastered façade. Brazil had caused the façade to crumble and the ensuing flood had almost drowned me.

In those few short weeks of regular meditation, I began to trust the certainty that when I felt emotional pain, it would pass. In the past I had been scared that if I allowed myself to feel deep sadness, then it would consume me. I had been incubating a kind of hidden depression. It was liberating to feel whatever I needed to, without fear of sinking so deep that I wouldn't recover.

I realized that our emotional state can change in an instant, just as a storm can pass from thunder to sunshine in minutes. I felt free to feel it all, knowing that I wouldn't become it.

In my urgency to stabilize the foundations of belief on which

I sat, I also read and researched. I began to discover a body of literature that talked of the 'mind-body' connection. I read about how our thoughts can influence our body and our health. I discovered books written about our various energetic or astral bodies. I found that scientific trials had proven the influence of our mind over our health. I read stories of how people with terminal cancer had cured themselves, just through visualization and the application of positive thoughts. I realized that what I had experienced in Brazil wasn't perhaps so bizarre or unusual after all. It was just a domain of experiences that were new to me.

I wanted to live my life being always true and honest to myself about how I felt. I would try and stay aware of my thoughts. Never again would I put on a mask. I didn't want to block anything inside me any more. I didn't want to judge myself when I felt sad or frustrated. I didn't want to feel the need to always be up beat. I didn't want to be battling with my own emotions. I was willing to feel them. I wanted to always trust that they would pass and that the sunshine would keep coming out again. I discovered this was all easier said than done. It is perhaps a lifetime of work.

In the meantime, I prepared myself for the adventure of Maui.

CHAPTER 16

MEETING THE RUSTY KNIFE AGAIN

"In every corner of my soul, there is an altar to a different god."

FERNANDO PESSOA

When I wheeled myself out of the airplane I was hit by delicious heat. It was a welcome change from the icy fingers of a Scottish winter. Bright floral scenes met me – colourful printed shirts, garlands of flowers and smiling people. Ken was amongst the crowd, not long arrived on his flight from Utah. Just seeing him was an immediate anchor to my experiences in Brazil, reminding me that I really hadn't imagined it all.

In a hire car, we negotiated our way to Joe's place, my senses agog at the colours and scenery. I had learnt about Hawaii's basalt volcanoes in my years of geology study, but it was impressive to see the long steady slopes of Maui's largest volcano, Halkadiki, rising from the sandy shore. It was a giant cone, towering over the miniature footprint of civilization that hugged the coastline. Guavas hung from roadside trees and avocados lay on the ground, a paradise feast oozing from 'Mother Maui' (as the locals called it). I was going to enjoy this trip!

A round of mobile phone calls and we discovered that Joe and other friends of Ken's were all at a party along the coast. We cruised along the shoreline, the golden strip of sand interrupted by impressive glass-fronted houses, low-lying hotels and golf courses. The urban sprawl died away leaving a naked, convoluted rocky shore. The air felt crystal clear in my lungs and the Pacific panorama stretched to silhouettes of other small islands dotted across the horizon.

We arrived at the party, a floating, colourful gathering of dresses and white cotton. The rooms were filled with tanned, smiling people. Everyone seemed so healthy and happy. Huge windows looked over the sea with lengths of neatly mowed lawn curling over the shore.

In the house full of strangers, a striking girl asked, "You're not Karen Darke are you?" "Yes?" I responded inquisitively.

With an amazed shriek of laughter she claimed "Your mum used to teach me at junior school in Yorkshire!"

What a small world. I felt instantly more at home in her company and with another Yorkshire accent.

It was great to see Joe. His gentle reassuring nature and hospitality eased me into life in Maui. He welcomed both Ken and I into his home, which became the perfect setting for the Fritz endeavours that soon began.

I was settled and enjoying the island paradise. I'd almost forgotten my reason for coming, until one week after my arrival we went out for an early dinner in preparation for the evening that was planned.

"Could you hurry the food along please? We've got an operation to go to," Joe asked pleasantly. The waiter hesitated, and gathered his confused expression for a polite "Certainly". Rubens smiled at me across the table. I took a bite of bread and swallowed a lump of apprehension with it.

It was now two months since my first operation. A quick scan by Fritz since my arrival in Maui had diagnosed that his first operation had shifted my subtle energy bodies, but that it had not worked back to the physical. "At least two more surgeries will be necessary in order to get the nerves communicating". The second operation was scheduled for tonight, after dinner.

I had left Britain to sceptical voices. "It's impossible"; "Sounds weird to me"; "He's stringing you along. How much is it costing you?"; "Well the first operation didn't change anything did it!" I deflected the negative comments, which were mirroring my own negative, sceptical voice. That "How?" part of me was stamping and screaming louder than ever. "How on earth do you think this spirit surgeon is going to get you to walk when all the doctors in the world can't?" But as far as I could see, I had little to lose, and everything to gain. If thousands of people were regularly operated on, and there was no history of anything going wrong, then I was willing to trust him. I'd decided to commit to another consultation and see where things led. It was costing me nothing except a few scars.

There was no charge for Fritz's services, though I'm sure the really sceptical people I knew didn't believe that. I'd discovered through sharing with people the story of Brazil, that if people really don't want to believe something, if it challenges their framework of beliefs too harshly, then no amount of convincing or fairly clear evidence will change their mind. If we're stuck in a river of thinking, it takes a serious jolt, and perhaps a personal experience, to burst us out of it and see things from a different perspective.

As I sat at the dinner table considering the evening ahead, my mind wandered once more. "This has to be the most bizarre situation I've managed to get myself into yet". I picked at my food, my appetite lost for obvious reasons. The last surgery had been completely painless with no bad after-effects and I could find no reason, apart from the obvious fear of being cut open again, not to proceed with the second operation – especially given the possible prize of the outcome. My nervousness hung over the dinner table like mist over the sea. I sensed an ocean of possibility but it wasn't quite visible. Like the captain of a ship, I was eager for the fog to clear.

Our small group gathered in the improvised operating theatre. It was Joe's garage with a sheet draped over a massage bed. I lay face down on the bed, feeling peculiarly calm, in contradiction to the apprehension of earlier. We fell quiet as Rubens sat, closed his eyes for a few minutes, and left to be replaced by Dr Fritz.

"Zo!" He exclaimed with a guttural Germanic voice when he saw me. He smiled, and with his characteristic mannerisms, reached out to tickle my ear. "Don't worry. Have God in your head. Let's begin." He switched into professional mode.

The first time Fritz told me "Have God in your head" was in Brazil. It had meant little to me, but my experience there during the operation was unexpected – beautiful, peaceful, pure – somehow divine. Since then I'd felt a sense of connectedness, perhaps just with myself. God had become a word that humanized for me the concept of the intangible: this place of peace, calm and bliss that I had found for myself. It seemed unexpected under the circumstances. To hear Fritz say these words again acted as a trigger for me to enter a similar state of serenity. I imagined that bright white light illuminated our small group as I felt the cold tip of his scalpel between my shoulder blades.

How Fritz did what he did seems unimportant. People might argue that he induced a hypnotic state in his patients. That his work was nothing to do with an external concept of God at all, just a connection with a peaceful relaxed place in oneself. But maybe the ability to be content, calm, relaxed and loving within oneself is all part of what God is. And those are all emotions that I have never experienced more intensely than whilst being operated on by Fritz. That is why it felt right to be there. I guess using the word God just depends on how we define it for ourselves. Maybe it is just a word that humans invented to describe something sensed, yet indefinable.

Back in the garage something in my mind said "Oh no! I can feel the blade. What am I doing?!"

My heart said, "Calm. It's all right. You know this is okay, and it won't hurt."

My hands were being held by Joe and Ken, and serenity swallowed me. I realized the cutting had begun, and once again, despite the lack of anaesthesia and the location of this operation, above my level of sensation, I couldn't feel a thing. The doubting part of me was reassured.

Fritz's surgeries reminded me of visiting the dentist, when my mouth had been numbed and my teeth were being pulled. It was a sensation of knowing that he was cutting and pulling my tissue, but feeling nothing. Occasionally I felt something that wasn't quite numb, and Fritz would stop and ask me, "Pain?" It wasn't painful at all, but each time he seemed to focus more and somehow

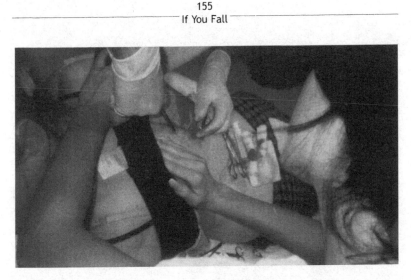

Surgery on my spine by Dr Fritz, Maui, January 2001

removed any inkling of sensation again. He explained that he created an anaesthetic effect by using subtle energies channeled from the 'Universal Force' in order to prevent pain.

He dug deep in the area of my thoracic spine. He was working higher than in the first operation. I heard a chinking sound as he hammered something metal into my vertebrae. He gruffly muttered "Bleeding. Stop. Stop bleeding!" Then he was calm again as apparently the flow subsided.

"What are you doing?" I asked, suddenly with a desire to take more interest in the activities going on in my back.

"I want to align the vertebrae. Move the spine across, to help the nerves repair." His answer for once made some level of conventional anatomical sense. I knew my vertebrae had been offset in the fall.

"Aaaaaagggghhh" he made an effort-laden groan like a heavy-weight lifter. He was pulling his whole body weight over the metal implement embedded in my bone. I still felt calm and peaceful, no pain. "Let go of her hands. Now move them, move your fingers!"

"Oh my God" was all I could think.

"Trust. Be calm" was all my heart could say.

The gathering around the table bubbled with excitement as they watched my bum muscles twitch and my legs kick. The movement was rapid and quite strong.

"Wow Karen. Your legs are really going." Someone around the table conversed.

"That's normal. I get muscle spasm all the time," I replied, unruffled and rational.

"Good. Excellent!" Fritz exclaimed. "This is good. A good sign."

My surgeon was apparently pleased. I didn't get excited about my jumping legs though. They did it all the time, especially when my body was being touched or moved in some way.

"You will probably need another operation, higher up in the neck," Fritz said, again tickling my ear and smiling at me kindly. "Now, stitch her up."

Dr Fritz apparently doesn't like stitching, so he left the qualified members of our group to do the work. Meanwhile he dabbled with a few other people – a needle in the chest for asthma, a hammer in the coccyx area for back pain. I lay there, in a cocoon of my own, blissfully relaxed.

"Ow!" I couldn't help but release a yelp as I felt a needle stab my skin. Fritz had just painlessly crow-barred my spine and now Ken was stitching me I suddenly felt pain. It put the previous thirty minutes of surgery into perspective and I was reminded intensely of the extraordinary nature of Fritz's work.

Whatever the outcome, I felt privileged to have experienced

it. I liked that I'd engaged with something that I previously would have found so absurd, inconceivable and beyond my beliefs.

As Fritz heard my yelp, he came over and stopped the stitching. He patiently taught Ken how to hold an index finger at each end of the incision and visualise energy spiralling in. "Now continue. No pain now." Ken did as Fritz said, and sure enough, I felt nothing.

"Good. Rest for four days. Now Rubens will be tired. I must go. See you next time."

"You're not an easy man to track down!" I chased.

"I will find you" he assured me. With a last tickle of the ear, he sat down. Rubens returned from some mysterious dimension, but left the garage immediately. He apparently didn't have a stomach for medical procedures. Odd considering what his body spent so much time doing.

The first incision had only required twelve hours of rest, but this incision was twice as long, about five inches in total, and the surgery deeper. I felt stiff between my shoulder blades, and I had no inclination to move. The group transferred me onto a proper bed by lifting me in the sheet so that I wouldn't have to move.

I slept soundly.

CHAPTER 17

MY DIVINE SPINE

*"People travel to wonder at the height of mountains, at
the huge waves of the sea, at the long courses of rivers,
at the vast compass of the ocean, at the circular motion
of the stars; and they pass by themselves without
wondering."*

ST AUGUSTINE

Within a few days, the stiffness disappeared completely and I felt un-tampered with.

I was soon fully active again. Far too soon.

I laid on immaculately mown grass, crashing surf battering the shoreline, and watched the sky light up a deep orange as the evening sun dissolved into the Pacific. The moon rose in perfect complement. Shadows of palm leaves rustled and a light evening breeze brushed my cheeks. I'd cycled, on my hand-bike, sixty kilometers along Maui's western shore. It has been a hot windy day, the front of my legs catching pink stripes as I pushed through a headwind in the high sun.

It was only four days after my surgery.

I had kept cycling in search of some wilderness which I was sure must exist somewhere on the island, but by six in the evening and a rapidly approaching darkness, I was forced to give in to the sprawl of hotels and tourist developments, and find refuge for the night somewhere.

After some searching, I settled for the edge of a golf course as the most secluded, peaceful overnight camp spot I could find. I had a short sleeping mat and a sleeping bag tied beneath my hand-bike. I selected a patch of manicured lawn at the edge of the golf course with the hope that the leafy hedge would obscure me. I awkwardly clambered down from the bike onto the ground and nestled into my too-thin, tissue paper sleeping bag for what threatened to be a long night. I was thankful that the air was still warm. It was only about seven in the evening.

As the orange glow of the sky faded a bright swollen crescent of moon crept higher. I turned on my head-torch and pulled out a book I had bought the previous day. *The Power of Now* by Eckhart Tolle. I read to the sound of the surf beyond the far edge of the golf course. My eyelids felt surprisingly heavy for such an early hour. Each paragraph was packed with such an intensity of words that I felt I needed a week to digest each page. But I was captivated by what he wrote. One paragraph in particular caught my attention and intrigued me, jolting me back from any lull into slumber.

"The reason why some people love to engage in dangerous activities such as mountain climbing, although they may not be aware of it, is that it forces them into the Now – that intensely alive state that is free of time, free of problems, free of thinking, free of the burden of the personality. Slipping away from the present moment even for a second may mean death. Unfortunately, they come to depend on a particular activity to be in that state. But you don't need to climb the north face of the Eiger. You can enter that state now".

Eckhart Tolle, *The Power of Now*

His words made so much sense to me. Climbing had been so absorbing. It had demanded complete focus. I could never be anything but acutely present, my hands and feet reading the rock face as if it held Braille messages. It insisted on steadfast presence. Anything else had been obliterated from my mind whilst climbing. Except for the precision and detail of each moment. It had made me feel intensely alive.

I already knew that it was painful to live with memories. It wasn't helpful to allow myself to be slave to them. It just meant being a slave to the passing of time. Resisting change. A prisoner of my own past. That was what could hurt so much.

But the practice of being completely present, not allowing oneself to indulge in the regrets and losses of the past, seemed so much harder. It was impossible to just erase it all from my mind. Yet I realized that if I could, then I wouldn't have the memory of walking. I wouldn't be able to compare now with then, to wish for something I didn't have. I wouldn't feel the need to pursue the desire to walk again.

Maybe that was why I was so addicted to adventure and physical endeavours. They required my total commitment and attention. They allowed me to connect with each moment, with the here and now. Whilst engaging in sport and adventurous journeys, there was so much to absorb myself in. In those moments, I was distracted from painful memories. At those times, I was always present, contented and at peace.

"But you don't need to climb the north face of the Eiger. You can enter that state now".

"Well, I can't climb the north face of anything anymore, so it would be great if I could enter that state now" I thought. "But I also don't want to stop having adventures. I enjoy them too much, though it would be good to feel that alive and engaged with each moment all of the time".

I lay the book down, switched my head-torch off and turned to stare at the black sky, jeweled with stars. "Just be in each moment", echoed around my head. I felt the muscles in my back relax into the ground and began to daydream. My mind took me up to a golden moon in a dusk blue sky, and I watched myself dive off its crescent into a calm turquoise Hawaiian ocean, deep into the blue. Then I walked through shoreline waves onto a silver-sand beach.

Spots of rain startled me, pitter-pattering on my sleeping bag. I sat bolt upright, aware that only a few drops would instantly soak my thin, warm cocoon. My hand fumbled for the zip, eager to release myself from the confines of the bag. I looked up at the sky and was confused to see its expanse of jewels still glinting. Where were the clouds? Was it just a small shower?

In sleepy confusion I lay back onto the grass. Seconds later I let out a surprised yelp as another heavy shower descended on me, first over my head, and then splattering along the length of my body, beyond my feet. Sprinklers! Golf course! Of course! What a stupid place to sleep!

An energy I hadn't experienced all day surged through me as I gathered my sodden belongings, stuffed them into bags and desperately fiddled to tie things onto my bike. I climbed into its squelching seat, the artificial rain drenching me at rhythmic intervals. I cycled away, over grass that had earlier felt as hard as tarmac and now felt like mud. I wasn't sure whether to laugh or cry. I glanced at my watch. Ten o'clock. Every part of me and my belongings was wringing wet. I chuckled, and then groaned.

I made a new camp on an extremely undulating and uncomfortable patch of lawn belonging to a doctor's surgery, and lay shivering as the warm Pacific night took on a chill. I abandoned any attempt at sleep and decided that the only way to stay warm was to keep moving. I clambered back onto the bike and dripped my way through the streets of Northern Maui. One fading head-torch light was my only warning to the growling super-sized engines that rumbled by, drinkers and holiday-makers finding their way from bars to beds. People lubricated with alcohol jeered and shouted as I dribbled past them, the strange silhouette of my bike a surprising sight.

Hours and hours passed as I retraced my steps back along the western shore of Maui. It was the most direct route I could take back to warmth and dryness. I cycled alongside the pounding surf, tumbling shells and pebbles, and through fields with sweet smells of sugar cane. And I pedalled through surges of adrenaline as the roar of four-wheel-drives gurgled by.

I stuffed energy bars into my dry mouth, their chewy, glucose-bound oats and nuts making me drier and my throat burn for more with synthetic hunger. Of the litres of water that I had on me, only a few mouthfuls were drinkable, the rest soaked into the fibres of my clothes and sleeping bag.

The sun began to rise, a salmon and orange streaked sky climbing slowly over the volcanoes, as if the giant black cones were erupting. I felt alive. Intensely alive. I was fighting a mini battle of survival. It demanded my complete attention. As the sun rose higher, I knew I had won.

Warmth and relief began to wash my body. The familiar towering neon strip of consumption that marks each US town came into view. It was six in the morning and I was running on empty. I decided to throw away my morals to satisfy my appetite at the first place open with food – a McDonald's drive-in. Something about going to a drive-in on a bike amused me. Fortunately, I was too low down to easily make the transaction and everything on the menu looked too unappetizing to satisfy my burning hunger. I continued, and soon found a small sandwich bar, its owner putting out tables and wiping them down. I sat in the golden morning light, feeling satisfied as the adrenaline eased from my system and the sun warmed my skin.

That night, I had been 'in the moment', totally immersed in cycling home safely through the darkness. I had felt intensely alive and alert – that state described by Eckhart Tolle. But I had merely replaced the thrill of climbing with the adrenaline of a cycling escapade. So maybe I still had a long way to go!

As the morning evolved, my awareness rose with it. I thought of all of the years I had spent since being paralysed, searching for sporting kicks, adrenaline, to bring myself into the moment. I realized that for as long as I could remember I had been looking for the short-lived thrill of these experiences and somehow I was never content. It felt like there was a gaping black hole inside me. What was the missing piece? I had spent years chasing in circles looking for a part of a jigsaw, constantly putting my life in danger, over and over again.

It was this very pattern that had got me into trouble in the first place and probably led to me falling off the cliff. If I hadn't been pushing myself so hard, desperate for more impressive physical achievements, then I would probably not have broken my back. It was as if I'd lost all balance and perspective in life, and then literally lost it by falling off.

For years I had been craving physical activity and adventure with a fury that kept me busy, occupied and externally focused. For all those years, I'd been looking for something, searching for that missing jigsaw piece. I had been looking for those moments where I was completely present, where I felt a connection to myself and some peace in all of the external chaos. In a world that seems to move increasingly fast, get ever-more busy, and be filled with more things – buildings, technology, consumer delights – it feels to me that the space and silence that each of us can experience is almost squeezed into non-existence. Being in nature, feeling the ocean's waves rise and fall, having time to notice the orange globe of a rising moon, the early morning mist blanketing a frozen valley...here I can experience the vast space and deep silence of the world. Being in these environments acts like a bridge that enables me to feel the space and silence within myself. Connecting with this allows me to stay balanced and sane, countering the speed and craziness of the world. It gives me perspective and a sense of calm.

I felt that I had just found a huge golden key to a door that led to liberation. It wasn't about changing who I was and my love of being physically active and in wild places. It was about finding balance in it, listening to my body and its needs, and being more connected with my gut feeling or intuition that I had ignored for so long. I had constantly overridden this feeling with my head, striving to push on, to achieve more.

I remembered just before leaving for Maui, sea kayaking off

the coastal cliffs of Aberdeen. It wasn't my favourite place to kayak as an eerie sensation haunted me whenever I was back in the shadow of the cliffs, but that particular evening it had felt stranger than ever. As we had teetered out of the harbour onto a bulging sea, I felt nervous and uncomfortable out there. It didn't make sense to feel so anxious. I'd coped with choppier seas before, and being in a double kayak we were relatively stable. But an unexplained sense of "I don't want to be here" nibbled through me. Only five minutes after getting on the water I had, for the first time ever, listened to myself. I hadn't over-ridden the instinct of "Stop!" that my body had shouted at me. I'd asked my friend Anne if we could return to the harbour and she had been happy to. She'd said that she felt nervous too. Despite the hours we had spent equipping ourselves for an evening on the water, I was relieved to be ashore. I was happy to have heard and acted on the danger I'd sensed.

I needed to do more of that. I needed to stop getting myself into dangerous places by pushing and driving myself into extremes. How did it help me to search for a feeling of being 'on the edge'? The long day and night I'd just spent on my bike were another great example. "You idiot," I thought "You have just spent the night cycling with one fading light through drunken traffic, sodden wet and hungry, with a four-day old back operation which really needed some time to heal!"

How stupid was I? How stupid can stupid be? Why had I made the ridiculous decision to explore the west coast of Maui on a bike and sleep on a wet golf course, all just a few days after a major spinal operation?

This most recent endeavour just highlighted the pattern that I'd been playing out for years. It was as though I had a total lack of respect for my health and wellbeing. I'd just repeated the very blueprint that had got me paralysed in the first place. One of being headstrong, totally oblivious to my body's cries for what it needed me to do, which in this latest case was to rest. I discovered when I got back from the ride that I'd split some of the stitches open, and I had to meet with needle and thread again. Would I finally learn my lesson?

Over the next few weeks I watched Fritz work on other people, and as I witnessed his incisions, part of me still found it difficult to believe that I had so willingly and calmly laid there whilst he had done major surgery on me.

The last time I saw Fritz in Maui, he looked deep into my eyes and said, "Have love, patience and faith. Remember to have love in your heart." He recommended that I wait a good few months between surgeries to allow the changes in energy to manifest.

I noticed a tiny part of myself guarding the gates of my heart, daring not to latch too tightly onto the hope of walking again, just in case of disappointment. I just hoped that the invisible forces that Fritz used kept working their energies on my spine.

I had risked. I had leapt into this new world of beliefs. I had given my body and my trust. I had reasoned that nothing ventured is nothing gained. I had risked before, in the domain of outdoor adventure, and discovered that often the result is something we never expected. Yet when the unexpected strikes us, in the disguise of disaster or disappointment, I have discovered that we can gain so much more than we ever planned. Whatever the outcome of this journey, it was one that I was happy to be on. I felt some acceptance for the uncertainty of where it would lead.

It seemed that my spine was taking me on a journey that

touched on divinity.

I recalled the title of my book on spiritual healing, *Miracle or Mirage?* "What is a miracle?" I wondered. "Does miraculous just mean that we don't understand it, can't explain it with the models and ideas that we have about the world? And mirage? Well, it seems to me that life is a mirage. If all that Fritz says is true, then there are many realities within different energetic dimensions, all happening in parallel. Maybe reality is just what we each experience. There is no one reality."

I enjoyed the nurturing cradle of Maui for another few weeks; exploring the island's volcanoes and coastline and the friendly, open nature of the people I met. I reflected on how fortunate I was to be there. In all of my travels I had been so lucky to encounter so many people who had shown me such kindness, and in doing so enabled me to get to all of these places on a shoestring. I remembered the people in Central Asia, who had so little yet had taken us into their homes and shared their limited food and water. I thought of the friends and family who had supported me back to physical and emotional strength after my accident. I appreciated the people I'd recently met, in Brazil, in Maui, and the unconditional kindness they had all extended to me. I wasn't rich in monetary terms, yet all of these things happened, thanks to me being blessed with resourcefulness and such incredible support and help from the people who touched my life. I felt thankful to have received all of this and I felt so fortunate for the surreal experiences of the last few months.

I began to understand what Fritz meant by "have love in your heart". If each of us could extend the generosity of our hearts to people we encounter, offering kindness unconditionally, what a wonderful place the world would be. I hoped that I would "do unto others as had been done unto me". Those wise words sounded familiar from somewhere! Regardless of my religious beliefs, there were certainly some golden gems of wisdom held there.

I felt part of a family, learning and supporting each other through a spiritual journey. Maui, it seemed, was a very spiritual place, one of the 'energy vortexes' that Fritz had spoken about – like an acupuncture point on the planet. Fritz was just one of the many healers to pass through Maui, and in my remaining weeks on the island I heard of other healing stories.

Ron and Merry were a generous couple who showed me great kindness whilst I was in Maui. They told me about a Philippino healer who stayed with them and specialized in back problems. They told me how she had parted the skin of Ron's back just by moving her hands through the air, then pulled out what she said was bad energy from his spine and threw it into a bowl of water. They'd seen a black cloud form a ball of 'gunk' in the water. Then the Philippino healer had sealed his skin over again, leaving no scar or sign of her work at all, and Ron had been free of back pain ever since.

I met Howard, from the deep south of North America. He described in his slow drawl how he could look at a human body and see it as a sack of clear fluid, with clouds or changes of colour where problems or blockages existed within its energy. I watched him work with an audience of locals, and he was able to recognize the pain or physical problems that some of them had and then apparently cure them as he spoke to them. With some simple arm movements and the power of his thoughts, he explained that he was moving their negative energy and returning them to a state of pain-free balance. Exclamations of surprise leapt from the audience as an increasing number wriggled their bodies, looking for the pain that they had become used to, then realizing that it had gone.

Between each of these healing melanges, I swam in the crystal seas of the island and devoured avocados and guavas that lay fresh on the ground. Maui felt to be a healing, nurturing paradise and I was absorbed by the whole new world that I had entered. My appetite for learning was enormous. It was as if I was building a brand new house of beliefs for myself. The foundations had perhaps started in the work with Leemac and were now solidifying.

My journey with Fritz had provided some possible answers about the vastness of the Universal workings that mankind struggles to comprehend. My other experiences in Maui seemed to add to the force of what I'd learnt. But if these explanations were true and the reality I'd lived with during the previous few decades of my life had been an illusion, then couldn't this all be an illusion too?

"I can only be where I am" I reasoned with my thoughts. "If it feels true to me now, then it is true for now. But it doesn't mean that further along the journey of life, this won't also become an illusion".

"Can we ever really know the truth? And is there only one truth anyway?" They were questions that have challenged minds for millennia, but it seemed to me, there were many ways of knowing the world.

I was sad to say goodbye to Maui and all the people I had become close to in those few months. I left in traditional style, with garlands of flowers draped around my neck. I carried with me the richness of all my startling experiences and an ocean of philosophical questions.

As the plane ate up the miles of blue back to Britain, the intense colours of Maui washed into the distance and I was left wondering how it would be to settle back into 'normal' life again. Whatever 'normal' might be.

CHAPTER 18

MOUNTAINS OF THE MIND

"You must understand the whole of life, not just one little part of it. That is why you must read, that is why you must look at the skies, that is why you must sing and dance, and write poems, and suffer, and understand, for all that is life."

J. KRISHNAMURTI

When I returned from Brazil I waited, desperate to see changes happening, to feel life creep its way back into the two-thirds of my body that was numb. I had felt pregnant with the expectation of regaining some movement and sensation. But now, on returning from Maui, I felt more patient, full of hope for what was possible in the mysterious tapestry of life, but less expectant. I felt calm. My return to Britain and my 'normal' routine weren't as shocking as they had been after Brazil, although I missed the sunshine and colourfulness of Maui.

I was interested though to do all I could to encourage energy back into the parts of me that I had ignored for so long. I set about finding a physiotherapist and began working my legs as much as possible. I pulled out an old standing frame that had been gathering dust in a corner, and began to stand every day, hoping

A **memorable mountain in the Karakoram whilst cycling down the Hunza Valley**

that the stimulation to my nerves and bones would help. I had a renewed interest in the health of my lower body and although the options of how to move it were limited, I did what I could, pedalling an electric leg bike and standing regularly.

For the eight years since my accident I had been trying very hard to accept my physical condition and to just get on with things. But I had also been denying the grief and sadness that was buried inside me. Encountering Fritz had forced me to take time to confront my biggest fear – my disability – and what it meant to me.

For the first time ever, I had experienced the raw grief of my loss. It was as if my whole being had been unblocked by a giant industrial plunger! All the sadness, frustration and terror of my trauma had begun to flush away and I felt a new energy surge through me in response. I began to question. When someone has an accident and damages their brain, they receive hours of intense physiotherapy, in an attempt to re-educate the damaged parts of the brain and re-gain some lost function. Why, when someone damages their spinal cord, part of the very same central nervous system, are they told to get used to the idea, and get on with a life without the use of their legs? It just didn't seem logical. What about the intelligence of the body? Was it not possible that with repeated movement, the body could re-establish pathways of communication, and find new ways of getting messages from the brain to the legs? Could the body not be capable of re-learning?

I used to think, "Well, the spinal cord is like an electric cable and mine has been completely cut. At the moment, there's no known way to repair it, so I'm afraid that's that. I'll never walk."

Now I was thinking "The body is intelligent, so how else might it be able to communicate? What else is in the picture that we're not recognizing? What might the body be capable of?"

At times, I questioned the apparent simplicity of my thoughts. It was tempting to ridicule myself and think that if there was really a way to re-educate the body's nervous system to walk after damage, that neurological consultants would have found it by now. But the shattering of my old beliefs during my encounters with Fritz had opened up a new world of possibility to me. I felt I had more choice than ever about what to believe, about what might be possible, and it felt like pure freedom to think this way. It was like the blanket that had been suffocating me for years had been lifted and fresh air, light with excitement and wonderment came rolling in. It seemed only sane to think of what might be possible, rather than of what wasn't.

I began to see that the medical paradigms of now will shift with time, just as my own belief system had shifted so radically. Probably in twenty, fifty, a hundred years from now, there will be solutions to the medical challenges of our time - paralysis, HIV, cancer. And maybe the solutions won't involve surgery, chemicals, stem-cells or biotechnology. Maybe they'll involve a shift of consciousness. A recognition of the innate intelligence of the human body and mind in healing, much like the Egyptians, the Greeks, and ancient cultures of our world practiced. I remembered Will's stories of the 'magical' powers of a small boy in a remote Nepali village, able to move a giant boulder that no crowd of grown men could shift. I wondered if somehow, in striving for knowledge and control of our world and the universe, we have forgotten how to use the most powerful forces and skills available to us.

I noticed when I returned from my experiences with Fritz, that some people didn't 'skip-a-beat' at my stories, and that others preferred to put them aside in a category of 'strange'. How many of us prefer to stick with our view of the world when presented with something that challenges it too starkly? How often does that mean we stay channelled in one way of thinking or viewing reality? I wonder how often that rigidity leads us to pain, disease or problems? I constantly question the view of the world that I hold, but try as I might to keep my view as broad as possible, it isn't always easy to notice the channels of thinking I've started to carve for myself. But wondering about it is a good place to start.

I was interested in what else was going on in the world with respect to spinal cord injury and repair, away from the mainstream focus of the medical profession, which was attached to repairing the spinal cord with stem cells or electronic gadgets – all interesting and valuable work, but not, I now believed, the only way. I scanned the Internet and journals and I discovered small schools of activity dotted around the globe. There was some research in France using laser acupuncture in combination with physiotherapy that was producing results, with some people regaining various degrees of function. There were physiotherapy centres in Switzerland and Spain using 'coordination-dynamics' theory, where with repeated movement of the arms, the legs could be pedalled, thus establishing some coordination between the upper and lower motor neuron centres of the body, stimulating the neural networks and re-educating them in how to communicate.

These various alternative approaches all involved long, hard work and commitment. But it still seemed revelatory to me that somewhere in the world, people with apparently completely severed spinal cords, which the medical mainstream believed to be irreparable, were regaining function and movement. In some cases, the ability to walk again, in others, the simple act of going to the toilet without aids. Amazing! How much is possible if we just think a little differently?

In the time that I spent with Leemac, and also with Fritz, I became aware that I had been searching. I was looking for answers, for something that would lead me to realizing the seeds of belief that had grown inside me about walking again. I was vulnerable after my 'crisis' and the mere suggestion of possibility was enough to send me in pursuit.

Experiencing the difficult change of paralysis was challenging for me. I had been thrown out of balance. I'd been catapulted into a state of grief and confusion. I'd looked outside of myself for answers, opinions, approval or resolution from the chaos that I found myself in. I had been searching to fill the holes of loss or dissatisfaction. All those years that I had sought to fill the gaping hole within me with another activity, a person or a theory. I'd found it hard to flow with the changes that life presented to me, not only in relation to becoming paralysed, but other changes too, with relationships and my career. It was always so tempting to cling to the old and the known that seemed to offer some nurture and comfort in times of change or turmoil. I'd sought comfort through relationships with other people or things, as if they held an answer to my problems, or an ability to fill my sense of lack.

Was I alone in this? Or do we all, when we fall, whether suddenly or gradually, play out similar patterns?

I realize now that nobody else has the answers for me. I am my own best guide, if only I can listen to myself. Trust myself. Be willing to act on what I sense I should do, in each and every moment. Then I don't lose the connection with myself. It seems that it is the loss of connection with myself that creates the need to find something in someone or something else.

Fritz had mentioned a third surgery, but as time passed, I felt less compelled to seek it out. I felt more content with how I was, full of belief that walking after a 'serious' spinal cord injury is possible, but with a sense that it would happen to me if and when the time was right. I didn't want to spend my energy chasing it like it was a pot of gold at the end of the rainbow, overflowing with salvation from this terrible thing called paralysis. It didn't really feel like this terrible thing anymore. Of course there are still moments and situations where I wish that I could just physically leap out of my chair or jump in the air for joy, but it doesn't feel like the terrible package that I once saw it as. It feels that I have finally come to some kind of true acceptance, rather than the false acceptance when I tried to play brave and convince myself it was all FINE.

I did meet with Rubens Faria one more time. We met in Glasgow, just over a year after Maui. He was holding a healing session, and I went along to seek out Fritz, and consider whether or not to go for the third surgery.

There is a small story I haven't told yet. Every person who has previously channelled Dr Fritz has died suddenly and youthfully, usually from an accident of some kind. Rubens had asked the spirit of Dr Fritz if this would happen to him, and he had been told that he would be in an accident in Brazil. Instead of staying around, Rubens went to Maui at the time that he was supposed to have this accident, and therefore avoided the death that he had been forecast. When I met Rubens in Glasgow, I saw no evidence of Fritz any more. He was working with acupuncture needles, in a very different way to that which I'd previously encountered, and his eyes, voice and persona were those of Rubens, not of Fritz. He explained that he was working a little differently, but asked me if I would like the third surgery, and suggested that I join him in Portugal the following month to go ahead with it.

Something in me didn't leap at the opportunity. I wondered if in Rubens choosing to avoid his 'scheduled' death, the spirit of Fritz was no longer being channelled through him. At least it seemed that he wasn't, or not in the same intense way. I thanked Rubens, and said goodbye, not sure whether I would see him in Portugal or not.

What Fritz's previous surgeries on me achieved physically began to seem unimportant. I valued what they had done for me mentally, emotionally and spiritually. The series of experiences had taught me so much and set me free in so many ways. I had found the belief to think differently and the courage to seize my life with my heart. I never went to Portugal.

I recently heard a story about a woman who was ill in

hospital with one leg twice the size of the other. She was upset, and sought support from a wise friend. This friend sat by her bedside and said thoughtfully "I can see you really do have a problem. You believe both your legs should be the same size." The woman roared with laughter. She immediately understood that it was her thinking that was the problem.

After my experiences in Brazil and Maui, I seemed more able to accept how I was. I was less judgmental of my situation against any thoughts of how I 'should be'. I somehow felt able to accept that I was paralysed, for now, and not wish for a state where I was not, but still with belief that it might be possible. I was left feeling free of the chains of regret or expectancy. I felt open to the possibility that paralysis might not be 'forever', but also able to accept what was, and thus life became a smoother, more enjoyable experience. I began to understand, perhaps, what Eckhart Tolle meant by The Power of Now. I felt freer than I had ever felt, of the past, and of the future.

I realized that I'd spent most of my time constantly looking backwards or forwards, even though I'd thought I hadn't! I'd spent time recalling good memories and feeling sad that I didn't have them any more. I'd spent time looking to the future, imagining what life could be like.

When I lay in bed after my accident, vividly reliving with all of my senses the memories of running over the moorlands, recreating the sound of hollow peat, of startled grouse, the damp smell of heather, I was creating pain for myself. It was painful because I knew that I couldn't do that any more, at least not in the way that I had done.

In the same way, when I lay in Leemac's room, imagining this perfect future where I could walk again, making it so intensely real for myself that I almost believed it were true, yet sensing a giant chasm between where I was and that picture of where I wanted to be, I created pain for myself. I was longing for something, for a goal that was a goal so far beyond my horizons at the time that it just didn't help me at all. It left me an emotional train wreck.

Part of my attraction to outdoor adventure sports is, I'm sure, about bringing me into each moment. If I'm focused on where I am rather than reflecting on the past or dreaming up a future, then I am closer to feeling content. It doesn't mean I have to abandon my memories, but it does mean not dwelling on sadness and regrets, and using the past to apply to the present. It doesn't mean I have to ignore the future. It means working to create my future now, rather than wishing and longing for an imaginary future. The outdoors offers me a form of escapism, not to mention the beauty and peace of nature. And what's wrong with a little escapism, especially if we are aware of what we're escaping from?

After Maui, I'd gone back to work, but realized that my passion lay in people, in how we learn and develop, and not in working as a geologist, although it's a subject I'll always find fascinating. I decided to follow this interest, and was lucky enough to move sideways within the company I worked for and work as a 'learning and development' specialist. That was where my passion lay. I was fascinated by the stages of learning and growth that we go through during the course of our lives. I wasn't willing to spend another minute of my precious life doing a job that I felt less than completely excited about. Life felt too fragile and too valuable. I wanted to enjoy each moment like a bite from a delicious guava, like those I'd tasted for the first time in Maui.

The more changes I made in my life, toward things that I was truly motivated and passionate about, the more immersed I could become. I seemed gradually more able to concentrate on the task in hand, enjoying what I was doing, rather than thinking of something past or something I'd like to occur. I noticed being able to 'be' in the present moment.

Through the saga of being paralysed, I found the work that I was passionate about. I became more aware of myself and of what I might be escaping from on occasions when I jumped on my bicycle or into a kayak. Isn't it often the case that through our difficulties we find our place in the world? We find the thing that we feel energized and motivated by, and through life's hardest challenges can come the greatest gifts.

Now I see that walking can be defined in more ways than the physical act. I am running in my heart for the first time in years. I haven't completely dismissed the possibility of physically walking. In fact, I believe it is possible more strongly than ever and I pedal my legs around regularly on one of the Swiss 'coordination dynamic' machines. It helps me stay healthy and only time will tell if anything else comes of it. Walking again is no longer a burning need inside me that consumes my thoughts, desires and energy. I do what I can to stay healthy. I do what I can to make my dreams come true, without missing the appreciation of what is now.

I believe that we have complete control over our life experience. We have enormous influence through the choices that we make, not just externally, but internally. How we choose to use our mind, what we choose to believe and what stories we choose to listen to inside our heads, affect our experience of the world.

But perhaps we don't have full control over our life situation.

Whether you call it fate, or destiny, there may be certain things that happen to us that are unexpected and can shoot like stars or bullets into our lives. Whatever transpires, we have the power to choose what to make of it. We can choose to turn our situation into a positive life experience. Or we can get stuck and experience suffering.

Maybe what controls our life situation lies in a realm that our thoughts cannot comprehend, define or understand – that mysterious something to which we feel reverence, awe, magic, spirituality and surrender. Our limited form of consciousness struggles to find words to define it – that thing we perhaps personify with the word God.

It is the reason I was paralysed. It is why Will died. It is why Scott walked. And now I accept, that whatever will be, will be. The unexpected will happen. What I can do is choose to embrace the challenges and to seek what learning might lie within them.

CHAPTER 19

HEAD, HEART & HANDS

"No creature can fly with just one wing. Harmony occurs when head and heart – feeling and thought – meet. These are the two wings that allow us to soar"
Adapted (non-bold) from a quote by DANIEL GOLEMAN

"Falling off mountains" is something that literally happened to me. And to my friends Will and Scott, and to numerous others since then. I see what happened to me, and to them, as a metaphor for the difficult and challenging situations that we all find ourselves in at some point during our lives. We all 'fall' in life at some point, whether it be suddenly and catastrophically or gradually through staying stuck in a situation that doesn't make us happy.

I believe that there is a gift in the fall. That gift will be something different for everyone. Only you have the answer as to what it may be, though it will likely take time to find it. I look back now and see how becoming paralysed cracked the hard shell of my ego. I had been so driven to push harder, climb higher, do better, and prove something to someone. I'm not sure who. It was as if I was unconsciously going about each day, driven by some bizarre force, completely engaged with the 'external' world and wholly ignorant of the quiet voice within myself. I valued achievement, courage, performance, and thus pushed myself toward those things.

But being shunted into crisis, my whole world, not just my spine, began to shatter. The more I experienced – from the accidents and deaths of others, to the world of spirits and healing energies – the more the world that I had lived in for two to three decades made little sense.

As my world crumbled around me, all the forces that lay dormant inside me were violently jolted. Hidden resources were shocked into action. I found myself able to cope with my un-expected and difficult circumstances more ably than I could ever have imagined. It was only the evening before I was paralysed that I uttered the words "I can't imagine anything worse than being paralysed. I'd rather be dead...". Our whole world can change in an instant. And we can be amazed at how we find ourselves able to respond. This has been my biggest lesson in how we underestimate what we are capable of.

It was only through experiencing all that came with paralysis, of being pushed to my limits by it, that I have learnt what I am capable of. It has given me a confidence and a belief to pursue things I may previously have thought I could never achieve. I believe that when our personal world collapses through some kind of disaster, major upheaval, suffering or deep loss, we are forced to confront something within ourselves. If we stay for too long in the rubble of the crisis, then we will suffer. But out of the ruins, we can build a whole new reality for ourselves.

Paralysis presented me with a choice; to focus on the loss and its sadness, or the new and its opportunities. Without memories, my new situation would not have been so traumatic and punishing.

But haunted with recollections of my life before it was turned upside down, I found it difficult to cast from my heart the bitter sharp pain of loss. I was filled with desperate loneliness. All I could focus on were the things that I couldn't do anymore, comparing new with old. I was stuck in my 'river' of thinking, my comprehension and imagination of what next limited by what I had known. I felt to be in a situation that was impossible to treat with indifference, but equally impossible in its rawness, to transform into something positive.

As I battled with my fears about my new situation, it helped me to have space to allow my thoughts to wander, from the clouds of sadness to the joy of a brilliant new sky. The vastness of the natural world and my relationship with it helped me to put everything into perspective and soothe the emotional highs and lows. Support from friends and family helped me to trust that I'd find the strength for the days and weeks to come.

The shock of Will's death and the stark reminder of my own survival helped me focus on the opportunity in my new situation. It helped me recognize that a stage of my life had come to an end. Before that I had clung to the past, was bound by it, and the meaning and enjoyment of the present was lost. As the mourning passed, I was able to lick my wounds and build a new life on the remaining foundations of the old. Maybe we can always find a reason to be joyful for what we have, even when it at first seems that all we have is ruins.

I believe that each challenge thrown at us in life presents us with this choice, to stay 'put' in a past, or with circumstances that no longer serve us, growing stagnant, lifeless and parched like a river run dry, or to embrace the change, jump into the torrent of the new and discover what beautiful lands it may lead us to.

Becoming paralysed caused me to question existence, transcendence, life, death, religion and faith. My brushes with death have been empty, at least to the conscious part of me, yet my explorations of spirituality have been deeply moving, convincing and revealing for me. I come away feeling small, but an important thread in an expansive web of meaning, connected in some way to a force that I feel, but cannot see. That force touches me whenever I am still and quiet – most often in the wilderness, but equally in a conversation with a friend or stranger that leaves me touched or reflective in some way.

I've wanted explanations, evidence, answers to those unfathomable questions of existence and meaning that haunt humankind. And I've been fortunate in my travels to find answers that make sense to me. I believe in a bigger picture for humanity, a kind of master plan in operation, and that life is an exciting journey of love and learning.

Ultimately, I believe the only way to live is to grasp the opportunity that hides in times of difficulty. I've discovered that sadness doesn't last forever when we walk in the direction of our heart. We can grieve and mourn for a while, as is only natural, but then it helps to move on and embrace the new.

It is helpful if we can learn to be attentive to the voices and instincts within us, no matter our fear, our ego, or the desires of our head. Forget what is 'proper', what is 'expected', what 'should be', and do what deep inside you feel is the right thing to do. As I've already mentioned, I don't believe I'd be paralysed if I'd been better at listening to those quiet voices within me; if I'd been better at living from a place where my thoughts and feelings – head and heart – could have met. If we can learn to join the feeling, intuitive side of ourselves with the more logical, objective part, then perhaps we can take action that keeps us walking a balanced and healthy path in life. In doing so, maybe we can avoid some of the difficulties that might otherwise hijack us. It's been a hard lesson for me to learn, the harmony of my 'head, heart and hands' – listening to and coordinating my thoughts, feelings and actions. I find it constantly challenging to trust and listen to those quiet voices.

What is more important to me now than ever is living the journey that has been gifted to me: being here, in each moment, living to the fullest and best of my abilities; being happy for what I have, and sharing that with others.

Whatever faith, religion or passion each of us may hold, what matters is if it can ignite in us sparks of meaning, giving us motivation and energy to enjoy the paths that we each walk. If we are happy in our own life we radiate happiness to others, and that is surely the greatest gift each of us can do for humankind.

Falling is part of life. We can discover the reason, blame ourselves, blame others, or imagine what might have been. But asking "What if?" is not important. What happened, happened, and so be it. Sometimes we need to follow the fear into blackness so that we can come through it and find joy in something won.

What matters is having the courage to embrace our fears, and listen to the quiet voices inside us, wherever they take us.

EPILOGUE

FULL CIRCLE

We shall never cease from exploration
And the end of all our exploring
Will be to arrive where we started
And know the place for the first time
TS ELIOT, Little Gidding

Summer 2003, a decade after falling.

"Paddle hard left." Voices fought to be heard through the foaming surf.

"Nose in behind these rocks"...

The shouts from the others on the shallow beach were lost in the rumble of surf-spun pebbles. Spray washed the salty tide marks off my spraydeck as we grounded the laden kayak, flinching at the sound of scraping fibreglass, relieved to be ashore and upright. We quickly popped our dripping spraydecks as the landed crew dragged us further from the reaches of the North Pacific. With the final double kayak landed, nine colourful paddlers exploded onto the steep beach – some went searching for the flattest bivouac site, others rummaged for straps and slings to begin carrying our kit.

Sitting awkwardly amongst the ocean-smoothed logs, voice lost in the roar of the petrol stove, I began making hot drinks and dinner. I called to anyone "Could someone pass me a water bag please," and then "And if anyone has a pan handy..."

Then I was silent, watching the others like busy ants unpacking kayaks, stringing clothes on trees to dry, splashing the salt from their skin with freshwater, constructing bivouac sites...the jobs that needed doing were endless, and I fleetingly wondered if we'd been too ambitious in believing this journey were possible, with two members of the team unable to walk.

The task we had set ourselves seemed enormous. We planned to paddle for three months and over a thousand miles, roughly following the route of the historical Inside Passage, a sea-journey along British Columbia's coastline to the fjords and glacier-draped mountains of Alaska. It was a journey I had dreamt of for years, but had never thought possible. I knew that my wheelchair wouldn't fit into a kayak, and had thought it too outrageous to manage for three months without my chair and mobility, completely dependent on others and in such an extreme wilderness environment.

This was the kind of journey I had dreamt of being able to make, especially in the months of working with Leemac and Fritz, when I had believed that walking again was the next thing in store for me. I'd imagined that being able to use my legs would make a trip like this possible. As it was, I was still paralysed, and I was reminded again, that with belief and determination, and the support of others – from good friends to virtual strangers – we can achieve almost anything.

Being there, in Canada's awesome wilderness, was for me one of those surprising miracles that are woven into every thread of life. How nine of us managed to find the space and time in our lives, as well as the motivation to coordinate the journey and to tackle a dream that had previously felt so outrageous, seemed to me miraculous. I relished each moment as if it were my last. I felt like a child, excited at the magic that surrounded us.

The first week was hard. Our muscles seared with the pain of overuse, kayaks and bodies groaned under the incredible weight of three months of food and belongings. But we learnt quickly, and our days fell into a routine, our rhythms dictated by nature.

The early risers in the team would entice the rest of us from our bivouac bags with drinks of hot chocolate and bowls of steaming porridge that were a lucky dip of chocolate chip nuggets or bland greyness. Half-asleep bodies would stumble amongst the log jams, gathering scattered equipment from hollows in the beaten tree trunks, stuffing kit into dry bags and generally mingling activity with quiet morning moments, one of the rare opportunities to sense solitude. Bound by the tidal rhythms, our days expanded into close to twelve hours of paddling, quickly followed by nearly twelve hours of deep seaweed surrounded sleep. Some days we had to force our eyelids into action at four in the morning and other days we could lounge until the lazy hour of eight, enjoying the cosiness of our sleeping bags. Eventually we could get on the water within just two or three hours of waking instead of the five-hour epics of our first weeks. We had learnt through experience, and the days became easier.

There were days when I felt fantastic, feeling the connection of my body, boat and blade, cutting through the water with ease. Everything felt to flow. Despite my lack of sensation or contact with the kayak via my hips, knees and feet, the subtle movements of the craft were transferred to my shoulders and I could read the sea by listening to my upper body. I felt intensely alive.

There were other days when I ached, when the next headland seemed to take an eternity of wind-battered struggle to reach, when negotiating a safe landing and making camp just all felt like too much effort. I felt intensely alive on those days too.

Our paddling odyssey came with its ups and downs, hardships and learning. Just like life. On the good days, the sun would shine brighter, the views would be more spectacular, the wind would be calmer, and a passing fisherman would give us a bundle of Coho salmon to cook on a crackling log fire. We would feel inspired and energized to paddle forever. On the tough days, the sea would chop, the sky was blanket cloud, the seaweed was extra thick, and we would get soggy couscous with dried carrot gloop. We would feel so exhausted that we noticed every metre of progress, or even felt to be moving backwards whilst paddling forward.

Our journey through the Canadian and Alaskan wilderness was for me a culmination and celebration of the years of challenges and learning that had led me there. The journey provided me with a space to reflect on the lessons that life had taught me in the preceding years – a place to wonder at the beauty and the miracles of the world that surrounds us.

For the first time since my accident I was able to be in a wild place and feel completely content. Of course, I wished that I could help carry the heavy kayaks or run into the ocean and feel its cool refreshment. But I didn't lament it. I didn't sit and stare and wish for what I didn't have. As much as the journey through the Himalaya had given me a sense of freedom, I'd still looked at the distant mountains and yearned to be amongst their peaks. This time I could just enjoy being in the wilderness, without longing to follow paths or climb to summits. I didn't have that niggle like a

Kayaking from Vancouver, Canada to Juneau, Alaska, summer 2003

pebble in my shoe any more.

Instead I noticed the detailed patterns etched in rich purple on the backs of the starfish, I heard the rocks of the shore amplifying the ripples and waves of the ocean. I heard deep gurgling laughter fill the silent air that blanketed the mirrored water cut by our blades. I felt the seeds of relief germinate as we slowly passed the crux hurdles of the journey – the tidal rapids, the open crossing, Cape Caution. I smiled at the sensation of paddling through swell big enough to roll my stomach. My body, heart and soul literally devoured every stroke of our thousand-mile journey north.

For all the days and weeks I had spent in mountains and wilderness, I had never really experienced it as I did on this journey. I had either been aspiring to climb something harder and higher, or lamenting what I could no longer do. But now, I could experience more fully the wonder that the world has to offer. I felt I had come full circle, back to the world of external adventure, but somehow changed, feeling calmer and with an appreciation that made it all even more special.

In Alaska, the mountains and their tooth-like ridges, incisor peaks, sheer rock faces and icy edges were a mesmerizing backdrop to the expanse of ocean, broken only by whale fins. There were resounding echoes as the whales slapped their tails on the water, plunging deeper into the sea. There were huge flocks of geese squawking in spectacular formations, sea lions grunting, otters playing and sea kayakers laughing. We paddled alongside an iceberg, and toasted Alaska with Bailey's on iceberg ice.

Quite simply, I felt more at peace than I had ever felt.

Now I live in the heart of the Scottish Highlands. The three-month journey through Canada was the start of a new chapter in many ways. I've since left my work with the oil company so that I can have more balance in my life and the time to do physiotherapy and stay healthy.

I run a small enterprise, Inspire + Impact, so that I can apply my skills and experiences in development training to support and coach others in making the most of life and overcoming challenges. I'm also involved with the work of Interventure, a charity I set up in 2002 to encourage and develop inclusive outdoor activities – that is people with or without disabilities – engaging with adventure and nature together.

We never know what is around the corner, but it is rarely what we expect. I just hope the next chapter of my life is as exciting as the last decade, and look forward to the learning and the journey ahead. You may wonder about my personal life of friendships and relationships, *of my ability to love and be loved, and of course there was a tapestry of these elements, which happened alongside the adventure part of the story that I've shared here. It is thanks to the depth of friendships I've been lucky enough to have, to the patience and support of my friends and family, and the generosity of strangers, that any of this has been possible.*

I wish you luck with whatever journey your life takes you on, and the courage and support to help you find the strength and passion within you, to take you wherever you dream of going.

For more information see

www.inspireandimpact.com

www.interventure.org.uk

A REMINDER OF THE

QUOTES THAT HAVE

INSPIRED ME...

"Life can only be understood backwards; it has to be lived forwards."
SØREN KIERKEGAARD

"When the morning's freshness has been replaced by the weariness of mid-day, when the leg muscles quiver under the strain, the climb seems endless, and, suddenly, nothing will go quite as you wish...."
'The Climb Seems Endless', Markings

"What doesn't kill me, makes me stronger."
ALBERT CAMUS

"Be willing to accept the shadows
that walk across the sun
If this world were a perfect place
where would souls go to school
Do not weep for the limitations
that you see existing in your world
Those limitations are there for a purpose

Where would there be an opportunity to learn
If not in the world of imperfection?
Do not grieve for those who suffer,
who are subjected to limited capactities for living.
View your world as a transient place
where souls choose to come
because this is what they have selected
as their mode of learning
to the most minute detail."
EMMANUEL

"There is no coming to consciousness without pain."
C.G. JUNG

"Even after the heaviest storm the birds come out singing, so why can't we delight in whatever good thing remains to us?"
'Even After the Heaviest Storm', ROSE KENNEDY

"There is only one courage, and that is the courage to go on dying to the past. Not to collect it, not to accumulate it, not to cling to it. We all cling to the past, and because we cling to it we become unavailable to the present."
BHAGWAN SHREE RAJNEESH

"You don't get to choose how you're going to die. Or when. You can only decide how you're going to live. Now.
JOAN BAEZ

"What we vividly imagine, ardently desire, enthusiastically act upon, must inevitably come to pass."
COLIN P. SISSON

"Sell your cleverness and buy bewilderment"
JALAL-UDDIN RUMI

"When one door closes another opens. Expect that new door to reveal even greater wonders and glories and surprises. Feel yourself grow with every experience. And look for the reason for it."
EILEEN CADDY

"From time without beginning, the tree of unknowing has been watered by the monsoon of mental habit.
What a tangle of delusion it has become.
Listen. Ponder. Practice. Chop it down with the axe of the guru's instruction."
CAURANGIPA

"...And I have felt
A presence that disturbs me with the joy
Of elevated thoughts; a sense sublime
Of something far more deeply interfused,

Whose dwelling is the light of setting suns,
And the round ocean and the living air,
And the blue sky, and in the mind of man:
A motion and a spirit, that impels
All thinking things, all objects of all thought,
And rolls through all things."

WILLIAM WORDSWORTH

"When the heart weeps for what it has lost, the spirit
laughs for what it has found."

SUFI APHORISM

"Love becomes the ultimate answer to the ultimate
human question."

ARCHIBALD MACLEISH

"The most powerful thing you can do to change the
world, is to change your own beliefs about the nature of
life, people, reality to something more positive...and
begin to act accordingly."

SHAKTI GAWAIN

"In every corner of my soul, there is an altar to a
different god."

FERNANDO PESSOA

"People travel to wonder at the height of mountains, at the huge waves of the sea, at the long courses of rivers, at the vast compass of the ocean, at the circular motion of the stars; and they pass by themselves without wondering."

ST AUGUSTINE

"You must understand the whole of life, not just one little part of it. That is why you must read, that is why you must look at the skies, that is why you must sing and dance, and write poems, and suffer, and understand, for all that is life."

J. KRISHNAMURTI

"No creature can fly with just one wing. Harmony occurs when head and heart – feeling and thought – meet. These are the two wings that allow us to soar"

Adapted (non-bold) from a quote by DANIEL GOLEMAN

"We shall never cease from exploration
And the end of all our exploring
Will be to arrive where we started
And know the place for the first time."

TS ELIOT, *Little Gidding*